ACCESS ALL AREAS
THE OFFICIAL COMPANION

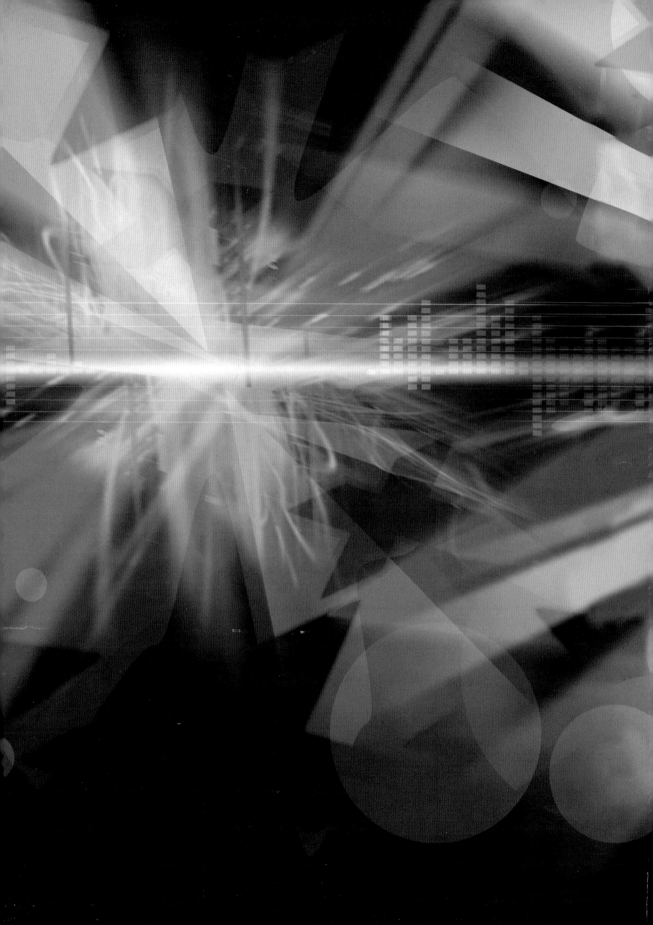

THE

FACTOR

ACCESS ALL AREAS
THE OFFICIAL COMPANION

JORDAN PARAMOR

headline

CONTENTS

THE X FACTOR FIRST HIT UK TV screens on 4 September 2004 and became an overnight success, attracting massive audience figures, swiftly prompting everyone from hairdressers to MPs to furiously speculate about who would be crowned the first ever winner. And with a £1-million record contract up for grabs, no one was speculating more than the nine finalists themselves...

The show was the brainchild of music guru Simon Cowell, whose aim was to find some of Britain's best untapped talent by travelling the country and holding open auditions where anyone over the age of 16 could come along and showcase their abilities. The panel of esteemed judges was to be made up of Simon, the legendary Sharon Osbourne and band manager Louis Walsh.

The show allowed groups as well as solo artists to compete and 50,000 people poured through the doors of various venues up and down the country in search of fame.

All auditionees had to impress the judges sufficiently for two out of three of them to give them a resounding 'yes', meaning that they made it through to the next round.

Once the lucky few were chosen, they had to endure what was affectionately known as bootcamp – where the aspiring singers were put through their paces and whittled down to 15.

By this time the hopefuls had learnt who their mentors were to be with each judge taking on a category each. Simon was awarded the Over 25s, Sharon Osbourne the 16–24s and Louis Walsh the Groups.

Once that process was complete, it was off to the judges' houses so the final nine (12 in Series Two and Three) could be handpicked to perform on the live show each week.

Suddenly Saturday nights came alive, with the nervous performers taking to the stage each week to face the public vote and the judges' sometimes kind, often harsh comments.

The live shows were played out in two parts; during the first episode the contestants would sing covers of popular hits in a bid to impress the audiences, while in the second – which was screened

was down to the public to decide who the overall winner should be, and almost ten million people watched to see who would be crowned *The X Factor* king or queen in Series One.

The show proved to be such a success that in 2005 it walked away with the Bafta for Best Entertainment Programme, beating the likes of Jonathan Ross and *Strictly Come Dancing* in the process.

The award was presented by self-confessed fan Ricky Gervais, and cemented *The X Factor*'s status as one of the funniest and most compelling shows on TV.

Since the first series the programme has gone from strength to strength with audience and voting figures increasing with each series – the Series Three final attracted 12.6 million viewers, while over 8 million votes were cast. The number of people attending auditions has also risen hugely, with twice as many people trying out in Series Three (a whopping 100,000) as in Series One.

There have also been a few changes to the format over the years. For instance, the number of finalists has risen from nine to twelve, and three acts now take part in the final show as opposed to two in the first series. The lower age limit was also dropped to 14 for Series Four.

Kate Thornton and Ben Shepherd left after Series Three and were replaced by the new presenter of the main show, Dermot O'Leary, extra judge Dannii Minogue and new *Xtra Factor* host Fearne Cotton. But ultimately the formula that has made the programme such an incredible success remains the same.

Since it first began both *The X Factor* and its behind the scenes spin-off show *The Xtra Factor* have grown steadily, and have become what can only be described as phenomenons.

The show has welcomed some of the biggest names in the music business during its four-year run, including Take That, Rob Stewart, Lionel Ritchie and Barry Manilow, while Iceland, Belgium, the Netherlands, Columbia, Kazakhstan, Spain and Russia now all have their own versions of the hit show.

an hour later – the two acts who got the least votes from the public had to sing to survive in a final showdown. It was then up to the judges to decide who stayed, and who went.

Once the competition got down to the final four, the eviction criteria started to change and it was solely up to the public to decide who hadn't made the grade. Each of the acts sang two songs each in the first live show, and when the act with the least amount of public votes was revealed in the second live show, they were told that their time was up – and no amount of grovelling to the judges could save them.

The Grand Final was crunch time, when the last two hopefuls went head to head to win the coveted record contract. It

SERIES ONE

THE EARLY STAGES

AUDITIONS

NO ONE REALLY KNEW what to expect from the auditions in Series One, but those hoping for an honest representation of the British public weren't disappointed.

The inhabitants of Leeds, London, Newcastle, Manchester, Glasgow and Dublin bless the judges and viewers with some of the least-talented 'talent' the UK has to offer. They include a man dressed as Spiderman, several sets of identical twins and a 67-year-old retired miner called Mario whose scary opera-style singing leaves the judges in stitches. 'I've never heard anything like that in my life!' exclaims a shocked Simon.

Louis tells one poor lady she looks like a drag queen, Sharon informs another she has 'seen better days' while a four-piece girl band are left in tears by the judges' comments following their performance of 'Dancing in the Street'.

Sisters Nancy and Jenny, a.k.a. Sweet Harmony, claim that they spend their evenings singing in clubs and holiday parks, but the judges have heard quite enough after less than a minute of their take on Robbie Willliams' 'Let Me Entertain You'. 'Individually you sound horrendous, together you sound even worse. I don't think anyone would pay to hear you sing,' Simon tells them. 'Oh, they do!' Jenny hits back. Hmmmm...

Sharon is even less than impressed, stating once the girls have left the room, 'They look like two ropey old strippers'. And she happily repeats her claim when the girls storm back into the room to confront the threesome.

But thankfully, in amongst the bonkers are the brilliant and finally the judges find some acts that they can put through to bootcamp. Law student Chenai garners a 'wow' from Simon Cowell and a resounding 'yes' from all three judges.

Another hopeful, Sharon – resplendent in a gold skirt and

glittery top – has come especially to see Simon. 'I've seen him in his trunks and he's gorgeous!' she tells the judges while Simon almost blushes. She even admits to having a Simon-lookalike boyfriend called Darren, who comes into the room to watch Sharon 'sing' 'I Just Called to Say I Love You', and turns out to be about two foot shorter than Mr Cowell.

Aspiring rapper Benjamin has all the attitude of a naughty schoolboy and, according to Simon Cowell, the charisma of George Formby. He feels the sharp end of Sharon's tongue after insulting all the judges, and she later justifiably threatens to 'put her foot up his arse'.

Twenty-year-old drama teacher Joanna is asked to leave the room when she tries to play her violin during her audition. But after reaching a compromise, she sings Jamelia's 'Superstar'. Unfortunately she takes her trio of 'no's rather badly, and has to be escorted from the room by Simon's man-mountain, minder Tony.

Thankfully, respite comes in the form of G4, who you may now be a little familiar with... The band walk through the door in their suits, and stun the judges with their

popera version of Queen's 'Bohemian Rhapsody'. 'You are an amazing singer. Amazing singer. Amazing singer. Really amazing,' Simon tells Jonathan, the unofficial frontman, while Sharon announces that she 'loves them'. 'You're a breath of fresh air for us,' adds a smiling Louis, relieved that someone had finally come along to break up the horror. The judges' incredible comments soon have Jon in tears, while Simon admits that he would happily give them a record deal there and then.

Identical twins Gemini don't fare quite as well when they perform the 'Boys of Summer'. 'Absolutely horrendous' is Simon's honest sum-up, before they flee in tears.

A certain smiley Steve Brookstein is next, but despite Simon liking him, the other judges are critical of his defeatist attitude. He gets a 'yes' from Simon and 'no's from Sharon and Louis – but is summoned back and invited to audition again the following day. Steve returns for his second shot, and, thanks to a good performance and a more upbeat attitude, this time he gets three nods from the judges. But there

are more scary hopefuls to come. A singing postman fails to deliver and is soon shown the door. He's followed by a terrifying woman who is told by Simon,

'You don't need a judge, you need an exorcist. Seriously, that was weird.'

Thirty-eight-year-old Stephen wants to 'tell the world about Jesus Christ and his love'. Simon soon has his head in his hands after what he describes as one of the worst auditions to date.

Girl band Diamante happily tell everyone that they're 'like sisters'. But when one of them, 24-year-old Adele, is asked to ditch her two 'siblings' and audition on her own as a solo artist, does she leave them behind in her bid for stardom? You betcha.

After numerous more not-very-good-at-all acts, the judges finally find someone to put through – 16-year-old Nicola who they think 'has potential'. And thankfully she's just the first of many.

Newlywed Samantha has cancelled her honeymoon so she could attend the auditions, and luckily her risk pays off when she gets into the next round. Just...

Former backing singer Rowetta blows the judges away with her voice. And even though they're a touch unnerved by her wild persona, she gets put on the bootcamp list.

There's only one person to round up the Series One auditions – a 144-year-old Princess Diana/Barry Manilow lookalike called Darren. 'I was born in 1860, I died in 1912 and was born again a considerable amount of years later and here I am now. I suppose you could vaguely call it reincarnation,' he tells the judges. Sadly, he didn't make the grade, but maybe he can help resurrect some of the careers of the poor people who didn't make it through?

BOOTCAMP

FROM THE THOUSANDS who applied, 114 acts have been chosen to attend the London-based two-day bootcamp stage. But with only 15 places up for grabs, it's set to be stressful and more than a little emotional.

The judges have been given their categories, and while Simon is at the Landmark Hotel in central London with the Over 25s, Sharon's at the Hackney Empire with the 16–24s and Louis is with the Groups at Angel Recording Studios.

There are mixed reactions when the contestants discover who their mentor is, but they're all determined to impress their allocated judge.

The first task for the Groups is to perform a song of their own choice which they've already prepared. 2 To Go are panicking because Louis wasn't a fan of theirs during their auditions, but thankfully Louis and his team love their performance of Disney's 'Beauty and the Beast'. Voices With Soul and G4's performances acquire positive raised eyebrows from Louis, but few are quite so lucky and after the first cull, many of the groups are heading home... In the afternoon they have to write and perform a song called 'Right Now', which has to include the words: world, dreams, hope, chance, anticipation and the phrase 'all the way'. They have one hour to do it

in, and after much deliberation, more shattered acts are sent home.

Over at Sharon's bootcamp, her acts are sharing a stage to sing sections of Stevie Wonder's classic 'Isn't She Lovely'. Samantha, who famously missed her honeymoon to go to the auditions, is worried about facing Sharon and her team as she was told to lose weight after her audition – but she's now seven months pregnant! Each of the 16–24s get to sing a verse of the song, and then it's decision time. Sharon is allowed to take 30 people into Day Two, but she's feeling tough and decides to allow only 27 through. The contestants take to the stage to hear their fate, and there's a mixture of jubilation and devastation from the hopefuls. Come the afternoon, the remaining contestants have a choice of two tracks to perform – 'Midnight Train to Georgia' and 'Love Grows (Where My Rosemary Goes)'. Poor Samantha forgets her words, but is soon helped out by her fellow competitors. Sharon crosses another person off her list, but soon realises that she's made a mistake cutting Chenai. She phones her and summons her back, telling her she's been given a second chance.

The ladies in Simon's Over 25s category are given the chance to wow Simon and his team first, by singing a song that

reflects their personality. And there are nerves all round: 50-year-old Verity sees *The X Factor* as her last chance at a singing career, 60-year-old Tessa is nervous as her last meeting with Simon didn't go what you'd call brilliantly, and 81-year-old Irene's in exactly the same boat. Once the ladies have showcased their wares, it's the guys' turn to perform. Steve Brookstein is first, while 38-year-old ex-*Brookside* star Danny McCall follows shortly after, and admits that he's hoping for a second chance at fame. When it comes to the cut, Simon only takes 16 with him, and although Verity and Rowetta are through to the second day, it's goodbye to poor Tessa and Irene, while Danny's second chance at fame falls by the wayside.

But only 15 contenders can go through to the next stage, and Day Two of bootcamp is when those lucky enough to make it find out the incredible news that they'll be getting the chance to visit the judges' houses – and may even grace the stage at the live shows. Day Two sees another series of performances during which many song words are forgotten and many tears are shed. But ultimately, those who deserve it triumph, while those who don't head home bitterly disappointed.

THE FINAL 15 have been selected, but as there are only nine places available in the live shows, the candidates are facing their toughest battle yet. Just three from each category will be triumphant by the time the judges' houses stage comes to a close – meaning that six of the acts will see their dreams crumble.

Cassie, Andy, Roberta, Megan and Tabby all head to Sharon's country retreat; Groups Advance, 2 To Go, 4Tune, G4 and Voices With Soul visit Louis' Dublin pad; while Simon takes Steve, Odis, Lloyd, Verity and Rowetta to his London abode.

Although they're excited about getting the chance to visit their mentor's homes, it's hard for them to relax and enjoy it because they all have one thing in common. They want success. And they want it more than ever.

At Sharon's, all of the acts have to perform in front of each other at her stunning mansion, while at Louis' impressive residence the Groups get the chance to showcase their talents for what could be the last time. Simon decides that he wants to get to know his hopefuls better, so he sits down for a cosy chat with each of them before making any decisions. He admits to Odis that he's the first one he would give a record contract to, while Lloyd tries to convince him that he would have no problem winning the competition. Simon's still wavering on unpredictable Rowetta, who doesn't help her cause by crying and acting as bonkers as ever during their brief conversation. There's also a sprinkling of tears from Verity who is worried that she'll let Simon down.

Yet it's not just the contestants who are in tears when the time comes for the judges to decide once and for all who will be in their final three. They each join their teams for a summing up, but Sharon's main issue is that she can't bear to let any of her acts go. Yet she knows that she has no choice. She decides to sleep on it and awakes the next morning with her decision made. After much soul-searching, she sits Andy and Megan down and tells them that she's sending them home, breaking down when she tells lovely Andy the sad news. In Dublin, Louis is still deliberating over his five groups, but eventually he makes his choice; he manages to hold back the tears when he tells Advance and 4Tune that they're not in his top three. It's a similar story for Simon – as, ahem, emotional as he usually is, somehow he stops himself from welling up when he has to let Odis and Lloyd down.

SERIES ONE

THE
LIVE
SHOWS

7/2143439

THE WEEKS RUNNING UP TO the big *X Factor* final were everything audiences hoped they'd be. Week after week the acts battled it out in a bid to make it to the Grand Final, and you could almost smell the tension in the air!

Among the more, ahem, interesting moments were the infamous time Kate Thornton ended up chasing Rowetta around the stage, Sharon's not-so-secret feud with Steve Brookstein and everyone's shock when, week after week, they found themselves loving G4 more and more.

It's always tough to be the first one out, but someone has to be, and the first live show saw Sharon's Roberta and Louis' Voices With Soul go head to head. Only one act could stay in the competition, and while Louis was voting for his, not surprisingly Sharon plumped for hers. Simon had the deciding vote, and he didn't take long to decide that he was to save Voices With Soul, meaning that we had to wave goodbye to poor Roberta.

Verity was the second contestant to go, while the third show saw 2 To Go voted off.

Week 4 saw Voices With Soul leave the show having been saved twice before, and in Show 5 there were a few

problems when it came to deciding who would go... With Cassie and Tabby up against each other after scoring the lowest viewer votes, both Simon and Louis decided that Cassie had sung her last *X Factor* song. But Sharon, who was mentoring both of the bottom acts, refused to cast her vote and say who she wanted to leave the contest. But unfortunately it didn't make any difference as Cassie's fate was already sealed and she was soon sent on her way.

The sixth week of the live shows saw crazy but fabulous Rowetta go, and before you could say 'Blimey, who's going to win?' we'd reached the semi-finals. The judges had one act left each when it came to the penultimate show, but not all of them were going to be lucky enough to have one in the final – someone was going to fall at the final hurdle.

Sadly it was Tabby who lost out, meaning that Simon and his act Steve Brookstein and Louis and G4 were set to go head to head in the big final...

23

THE GRAND FINAL

AFTER EIGHT NAIL-BITING WEEKS, it's time for the final. And with that all-important £1-million record deal up for grabs, finalists Steve Brookstein and G4 have got to give their performances everything they've got – and then a little bit more.

Dressed in a gorgeous gold sparkly dress, host Kate Thornton bounds on the stage while the excited audience clap, scream and whoop as the night's proceedings kick off.

There was genuine, full-blown rivalry in *The X Factor* studio – and not just between the two acts. It's no big secret that Steve and Louis don't get along, while understandably Simon is in his corner and thinks that Louis has been fighting dirty. Simon and Steve come onto the stage and Simon announces, 'By the end of tonight I will wipe the smug smile off Louis' face.' G4 and Louis then step onto the stage, and Louis retaliates to Simon's comment by saying that he wants to take the smug smile off Simon's face. Let the battle commence...

Steve is the first to perform and belts out '(Your Love Keeps Lifting Me) Higher and Higher', backed by a full choir, to a jubilant crowd which includes celebs like Sarah Ferguson, Princesses Beatrice and Eugenie, TV presenter Sally Mean and all of the show's finalists.

Next up it's G4 with their beautiful rendition of 'Nessun Dorma', and there isn't a dry eye in the house.

Steve soon takes to the stage again, and he slows things down for a heartfelt performance of 'Smile'. Louis manages to get past his obvious dislike of Steve by graciously saying that both of his performances were 'Good, very pleasant, very nice' while Sharon cuttingly says, 'I'm going to use a quote that you used about your girlfriend – "You to me are like a Volvo. Reliable".' Ouch.

It's time for G4's second song, and they pull their trusty and brilliant

'Bohemian Rhapsody' out of the bag and perform it to perfection. 'Both songs, ten out of ten,' Simon tells them. Jonathan cries when Sharon labels him a superstar, and he extends the compliment to the rest of the band, telling them, 'I think we've all grown into superstars.'

Steve's third and final song is Phil Collins' 'Against All Odds (Take a Look at Me Now)', and then it's time for him to face the judges for the last time ever. He gets a mauling from both Louis and Sharon, with the feisty Mrs Osbourne saying, 'He's overconfident... He's full of crap and he's an average singer.'

There's some light relief when G4 perform their final track of the night, Radiohead's 'Creep'. And there are no harsh words for them as Simon tells them, 'You have no idea how much I wanted to hate that, but I liked it!' Sharon adds, 'They're endless with what they can do. Well done.'

After a break to count the votes, the results are in and everyone waits breathlessly while the winner is announced. After a tense pause and with over 9 million votes cast, Kate announces to a stunned Steve that he's the winner of the first ever *X Factor*. He and Simon share a hug before they both shake hands and hug a gracious G4. 'I'm shocked, shocked!' Steve grins.

The final performance of the series is from its winner – and as Steve smiles and laughs his way through another rendition of 'Against All Odds (Take a Look at Me Now)', we get the feeling he's rather happy with the outcome...

'Look how special she is.'
SHARON

Roberta Howett

Roberta started singing at a young age and is also a talented pianist, having played from the age of seven to 18. A career in music was always her dream and after leaving school she joined a girl band in her native Dublin. But when one of the members left she decided to take the plunge and go solo, and that's where *The X Factor* came in...

Roberta hoped that people would vote for her, saying, 'I have the "X Factor" because I put as much of me as I can into the song and try to connect with the audience every time.'

But, sadly, despite her angelic voice and stunning looks, Roberta was the first contestant to be voted off the show.

However, she's not one to give up that easily. She's still busy working on her music, and currently has 2,000 friends on her myspace page who regularly log in to check out her new material.

Age: 23

From: Dublin

Auditioned: Dublin

Mentor: Sharon / 16–24s

Audition songs: Ain't No Sunshine; It's Too Late

Judge's house song: Cry Me a River

Song sung at each stage of final:
1 Superstar

Final position: 9th

Vocal coach Verity had always dreamt of getting her big break. She left school at 15 to work on her local music circuit, and later formed a cabaret double act with her husband and together they toured bars and clubs.

She was dedicated to landing a record deal, and her hard work paid off when she was spotted while working and living in LA in the 80s. She was eventually offered a solo deal with Motown Records, but things didn't work out as planned and Verity later moved back to the UK.

It was a friend who told her about *The X Factor* auditions, but she was in two minds about applying so she left it until 4pm on the final day to ring the audition line.

Verity shared a flat with Steve during the filming of the show, and the pair soon became good friends with Verity regularly cooking him his favourite meal of, er, omelettes!

Despite loving her at the auditions, her mentor Simon Cowell later mused that he worried she was a bit 'pub singer-ish'. And sadly her rendition of Bette Midler's 'Wind Beneath My Wings' during the second live show failed to impress audiences and she became the next contestant to be eliminated.

Verity Keays

'You're too nice to be in this business because this business is tough.'
SIMON

Age: 50

From: Grimsby

Auditioned: London

Mentor: Simon / Over 25s

Audition song: When I Fall in Love

Songs sung at each stage of final:
1 I Will Always Love You
2 Wind Beneath My Wings

Final position: 8th

2 To Go

'I love you guys so much. You're so organic and there's nothing I can fault.'

SHARON

Peter Jones, Emma Paine

From: Nottingham

Auditioned: Leeds

Mentor: Louis / Groups

Audition song: Endless Love

Judge's house song: From This Moment On

Songs sung at each stage of final:
1 Don't Know Much
2 Always
3 (I've Had) The Time of My Life

Final position: 7th

Emma, 23, and Peter, 24, both started singing from a young age – in choirs at school – and became good friends when they were 16. Shortly afterwards they began performing together and were soon signed to a talent agency. Five years of gigging as a duo in pubs, hotels and social clubs followed before they decided to try out for *The X Factor*.

Peter, who has been blind since childhood, was considered the better singer by Simon Cowell, but he defended his partner saying, 'To hear someone say half of your band is not good is tough, but we've been singing together for seven years and if I didn't think Emma was great we wouldn't have lasted this long. In my book Emma has nothing to prove.'

Meanwhile, Emma hoped that their warm personalities would win people over. 'I hope people will see our natural personalities and how well we get on. We finish each other's sentences and know what each other is thinking. We hope they'd vote for us because they recognise our talent and our chemistry on and off the stage.'

But while the pair did win over the public during the series, sadly it wasn't enough to ensure them a place in the final and they became the third act to be voted off.

Voices With Soul

'I just adore you, I really do. Just three divas.' SHARON

Bus driver and hairdresser Grace, 42, her sister Hildia, a 37-year-old singer and IT student, and Grace's 25-year-old university student daughter Corene, wowed the judges week after week.

The trio had started singing together six months before auditioning for the show, performing mainly at weddings and church functions. Their ability to belt out old hits in an incredible soulful style (hence their name) made them an instant hit.

Hildia already had an impressive singing career behind her, having performed in the musical *Smokey Joe's Café* in London's West End, understudied for Chaka Khan and Mica Paris and performed backing vocals on Madness' 'Wings of a Dove'.

But despite their stunning vocal performances and popularity – Geri Halliwell admitted to being a big fan – sadly the ladies didn't make it all the way to the final. Along with G4, the girls polled lowest during the fourth live show when they performed 'Lady Marmalade', and the two groups had to face each other in a sing-off.

With all three judges deciding to save G4, it was time to say goodbye to the threesome. But the ladies have been kept busy with gigs and concerts since appearing on the show, and plan to release a single and album soon.

Corene Campbell, Grace Campbell, Hildia Campbell

From: Luton

Auditioned: London

Mentor: Louis / Groups

Audition song: Bridge over Troubled Water

Judge's house song: I Will Always Love You

Songs sung at each stage of final:
1 Ain't No Mountain High Enough
2 (You Make Me Feel Like) A Natural Woman
3 Bridge over Troubled Water
4 Lady Marmalade

Final position: 6th

Cassie Compton

Age: 17

From: North London

Auditioned: London

Mentor: Sharon / 16–24s

Audition song: His Eye Is on the Sparrow

Judge's house song: Anyone Who Had a Heart

Songs sung at each stage of final:
1 Alfie
2 Without You
3 I Say a Little Prayer
4 Hero
5 All by Myself

Final position: 5th

'You're going to be in the music business for a long, long time.'
LOUIS

Student Cassie already had a background as a singer and actress before auditioning for *The X Factor*, having performed in shows including *Whistle Down the Wind* (aged 10) and *The Secret Garden*, both at the Aldwych Theatre in London.

Cassie was hoping that people would be moved by her singing and said, '*The X Factor* to me is being able to sing and touch people with my voice – I love it when people are enjoying my performance.'

Although she didn't go all the way and was eventually eliminated three weeks before the final, *The X Factor* proved to be a massive stepping stone for Cassie and she has continued to have a successful career since the show.

Soon afterwards she joined Tabby to present an award to Kylie Minogue at the *Smash Hits* Awards, released a single, 'Bring the Walls Down', which went in at Number 12 on the official download chart, and in 2006 appeared in two episodes of the long-running drama *Casualty*.

She has also continued with her theatre work and in June 2007 she began a stint in the ever-popular West End production of *Les Misérables* playing Eponine.

Rowetta Satchell

Larger-than-life Rowetta kept everyone amused on *The X Factor* with her huge personality and booming voice, and reckoned she should win the show because, 'I have individuality, personality, unpredictability, talent, confidence and stage presence.'

After being inspired by Diana Ross at a young age, Rowetta had been singing for an impressive 25 years before auditioning for the show. She released two singles with a band called Vanilla Sound Corp in 1987, and then two solo singles, 'Back Where We Belong' and 'Passion'. She later spent 14 years as a backing singer for numerous bands, including Inner City, Simply Red and the Happy Mondays, famously singing on their 1990 Number 5 hit 'Step On'.

Rowetta admitted that she felt like the show was her last chance to find fame, and she went all out to impress the judges. And while she certainly did that (also leaving them slightly bewildered at times), sadly it wasn't enough to win her the competition.

However, she did bag a recording deal with Gut Records off the back of the show and released her first solo album in October 2005. In 2006 she appeared on the Children In Need show *Celebrity Scissorhands*; Rowetta still tours extensively throughout the UK and is continuing to work on new music.

'You have a God-given talent and Simon has nothing to do with it.'
SHARON

Age: 38

From: Manchester

Auditioned: Manchester

Mentor: Simon / Over 25s

Audition songs: Lady Marmalade; Bridge over Troubled Water

Songs sung at each stage of final:
1 You Don't Have to Say You Love Me
2 I Still Haven't Found What I'm Looking For
3 Over the Rainbow
4 MacArthur Park
5 Somewhere
6 River Deep, Mountain High; When You Tell Me That You Love Me

Final position: 4th

'Tabby's just a born entertainer.'
LOUIS

When Tabby says that he started out in music young, he's not joking. The rocker began performing at six, played to bar crowds at eight, and was in his first band by 12. His group, Petronella, released two singles in his native Ireland, including 'Feeling So Low', which made it into the Irish top thirty. He later formed another band called Boom before trying out for *The X Factor*.

He said that if he won he would, 'Give my son and girlfriend a huge sloppy kiss and then I'll thank God and Sharon on my hands and knees.' However, despite coming incredibly close to the final, he was pipped at the post by G4 and Steve Brookstein.

Following his exit from the show, Tabby appeared on the *Smash Hits* Awards with Cassie handing an award to Kylie Minogue and he also filmed a 'rockumentary' entitled *What Tabby Did Next*. It aired around the time of his first single release, 'Number 1', which went to Number 7 in the Irish charts.

In 2005 Tabby got to realise a dream when he performed at Liverpool's famous Cavern Club. He still appears regularly at gigs and festivals and plans to release an album in 2007.

Tabby Callaghan

Age: 23

From: Sligo

Auditioned: Dublin

Mentor: Sharon / 16–24s

Audition songs: Long Train Runnin'; Keep the Faith

Judge's house song: Maggie May

Songs sung at each stage of final:
1 You Really Got Me
2 My Oh My
3 Addicted to Love
4 I Don't Want to Miss a Thing
5 Sweet Child O' Mine
6 More Than Words; Livin' on a Prayer
7 Pride (In the Name of Love); Sailing

Final position: 3rd

G4

Twenty-four-year-old Matt, 22-year-old Jonathan, 23-year-old Mike and 22-year-old Ben formed G4 after meeting at the Guildhall School Of Music and Drama in London. The former buskers amazed the public and judges with their popera versions of hit songs, including Queen's 'Bohemian Rhapsody' and Frank Sinatra's 'My Way'.

The four-piece made it all the way to the finals, but were just beaten by Steve Brookstein despite an incredible rendition of Radiohead's 'Creep'.

However, the band soon landed a record deal and released their self-titled debut album which reached Number 1 in March 2005. It was top of the charts on Mother's Day and went on to go double platinum, selling over 600,000 copies.

They have released two further albums, *G4 and Friends* in November 2005, and *Act Three* in November 2006.

But despite their huge success, sadly the band announced in April 2007 that they were to go their separate ways and released a statement saying, 'To you, our fans, we appreciate that this morning's news that we are splitting up will have come as a shock... The decision that we have come to has taken a long time and is certainly not a decision that we have taken lightly and is a group decision, nothing to do with either the record label or management.'

The band's final performances together were during a farewell tour for their fans in the summer of 2007.

Jonathan Ansell, Mike Christie, Matt Stiff, Ben Thapa

From: London

Auditioned: Leeds

Mentor: Louis / Groups

Audition song: Bohemian Rhapsody

Judge's house song: Creep

Songs sung at each stage of final:
1 Everybody Hurts
2 Don't Look Back in Anger
3 ...Baby One More Time
4 Circle of Life
5 My Way
6 You'll Never Walk Alone; Somebody to Love
7 O Holy Night; Bohemian Rhapsody
Final: Nessun Dorma; Bohemian Rhapsody; Creep

Final position: 2nd

WINNER Steve Brookstein

Age: 37

From: Mitcham, Surrey

Auditioned: London

Mentor: Simon / Over 25s

Audition songs: That's Why; Part Time Love

Songs sung at each stage of final:
1 When a Man Loves a Woman
2 If You Don't Know Me by Now
3 Smile
4 Help Me Make it through the Night
5 Let's Stay Together
6 I Get the Sweetest Feeling; If I Could Turn Back the Hands of Time
7 Have I Told You Lately that I Love You?; Greatest Love of All

Final: (Your Love Keeps Lifting Me) Higher and Higher; Smile; Against All Odds (Take a Look at Me Now)

Final position: 1st

'Every middle-aged woman would love to spend the night with you.'
SHARON

'Steve is a great ballad singer... He's got this great confidence that I wish I had.' LOUIS

Steve Brookstein made history when he became the first ever winner of *The X Factor* in 2004 after scoring over 6 million votes from the adoring public. His cheeky smile and soulful voice made him a housewives' favourite across the land, and he saw off stiff competition from G4 to land the coveted £1-million record deal.

The X Factor wasn't Steve's first taste of fame – he had previously supported Dionne Warwick and in 1997 he came second on ITV's *Big Big Talent Show*, which was hosted by Jonathan Ross.

He was also no stranger to the music business having had a singles record deal with Sound Proof, MCA, back in 1996 under the name The Funk Essentials. The band consisted of Steve and his friend Ryan and their first release, 'Only You', acquired brilliant reviews and became Judge Jules' Record of the Week. But sadly disappointment followed when the record label closed down and the single was pulled from sale after just one day.

Several other potential deals followed, but for some reason they always fell at the last hurdle and Steve was left feeling disillusioned. But his passion for singing was so strong that he was determined to continue and would explore any avenue open to him.

He spent much of his time song writing and singing classic soul tunes in bars and clubs and at weddings and private parties, but it was still his dream to land a record deal. And when he was voted the undisputed winner of *The X Factor*, scoring two-thirds of all votes cast, he did just that.

He soon became a firm favourite and his fan base grew at an impressive rate. His first single, a cover of the Phil Collins' hit 'Against All Odds (Take a Look at Me Now)', was released on 8 January 2005 and instantly went to Number 1 in the charts. His album *Heart and Soul*, released on 16 May 2005, also went straight to Number 1, selling over 150,000 copies.

Steve split from his record company later the same year, but went on to form his own record label on which he released his second album, *40,000 Things*, in October 2006.

He still makes regular appearances on TV, featuring on *The Match*, *The Wright Stuff* and *Loose Women*. He toured the UK in 2006 and is currently working on a new album which he hopes to release in 2007.

What have been your best experiences of *The X Factor* to date?

Certainly the best was finding Leona Lewis and the fact that she won *The X Factor* Series Three. I was more happy about that than anything else. I just think she's incredible.

What have been the worst things?

Nothing particular comes to mind apart from all of the auditions. Not one in particular, all of them! I'm so bored of them and I really wish we didn't have to do them. The days feel like weeks, they really do. I'm beginning to hate them more and more.

Have you had plenty of weirdos coming along to the auditions this year?

Ninety-nine per cent of the people that we've had come in have been rubbish. Or weirdos. But honestly, I would rather have a weirdo than a non-entity. It's when someone comes in and sings 'Falling' by Alicia Keys and they're not as good as the original... That I can't bear. At least the weirdos are entertaining.

Are there particular songs that you hate hearing now?

Yes, 'At Last' by Etta James is a favourite, and a lot of people have been singing Amy Winehouse's 'Rehab' this year. In fact, I think that's the song that's been sung the most. 'Falling' by Alicia Keys is still very popular, and John Legend's 'Ordinary People'. The original is boring enough but people trying to emulate it is even worse. After a while you decide you can't hear any more.

Have you had people dressing up as chickens and the like?

Yes, but they're obviously the ones that just want to get on TV so I don't put them through any more. We make a point on *The X Factor* that everyone is genuinely talented and not just coming in to get noticed.

And if you're good enough, you shouldn't need gimmicks...

Totally. I always liked the fact that Leona was very shy and unassuming when she came to the auditions. She had a presence whether she knew it or not. I knew that Leona had amazing potential, but it happens a lot where the first time they perform they're amazing, and the second time they're nowhere near as

good – it can be very disappointing. I try not to expect too much so that I'm not disappointed.

Have you had a lot of people crying when they didn't get through?
Probably, but it usually happens outside the room. I would anticipate that a lot of people do because they want to succeed so much. No one likes seeing people cry and we would never upset people on purpose, but some people do get a bit overwhelmed.

How was it having Dannii on the judging panel this year?
It was an interesting process this year. Auditions are like having dinner parties because you spend so much time together, and all of a sudden someone else joins you and it's rather strange. I've known Sharon and Louis for a long time and I think Dannii was very suspicious of me when we first met. But after about a month it was perfectly fine.

Dannii is surprisingly feisty!
She's like a little Jack Russell – she snaps without you realising it. But she was very protective of me with some of the people who were rude to me, which I loved. What I love about Dannii is that she knows her own mind, and she's been an artist herself so she knows what she's talking about. And of course, she is very cute.

Have there been many rows between you judges so far?
Oh, nothing that you wouldn't expect. We did bootcamp together this year and that made me realise that we have very, very different tastes. It made me realise how out of sync we are with each other.

How is it having Dermot hosting the show?
It's as if he's been on the show since Day One. He really likes people so it's a very easy job for him to do. And he's one of the most likeable people I've ever met so everyone gets on with him.

Are you excited about this series?
Cautiously excited. You never know how good someone is until you put them on that big stage, and people can disappoint. Even Leona wasn't amazing from Week One – it was only on the third week when she sang 'Summertime' that she found her stride.

Did anyone blow you away in auditions this year?
The fourteen-year-olds have done really well. They're very professional and focused. And the groups are strong this year – one or two are the best we've ever had. There's a potential winner in every category.

Why did you decide to change the lower age limit this year?
I meet a lot of kids on the road and it struck me that fourteen-year-olds are now like eighteen-year-olds; it felt wrong to say they were too young to give it a go. It was really just an experiment but we've found some good talent.

How long do you plan to keep doing The X Factor?
Well, number one, we'll do it as long as people want to watch it. And number two, the talent levels have got to be huge each year. If we end up with a substandard show, there's no way we'll do any more.

What are you most excited about with Series Four?
The unknown. I like the unknown aspect of what people are going to be like in the final stages. And I like turning someone good into someone who's potentially brilliant.

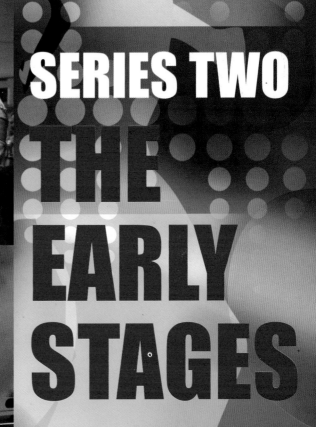

SERIES TWO
THE EARLY STAGES

AUDITIONS

BY SERIES TWO, contestants had got savvy after seeing the mauling that many of the hopefuls got from the judges during the previous series' auditions. So very sensibly they all decided to stay away. Oh no, hang on a minute, that's not what happened at all. In fact, it seems that even stranger people than ever crept out of the woodwork and along to the audition venues. An extra 25,000 people, in fact. Although to be fair, they weren't all bad. Just quite a few of them...

Then there was bad news for all those who weren't, erm, terribly good, because the judges had toughened up from Series One and they weren't about to take any prisoners. Some of the cruellest put-downs included: 'You should stick with your job stacking shelves in Sainsbury's' (Louis); 'Great cabaret but not for recording' (Sharon) and 'You've got to be kidding. That was loathsome – one of the corniest, worst auditions I've ever seen in my life' (Simon).

But while the judges were still being mean to the auditionees, they promised to keep their own egos in check to avoid the kind of disagreements they'd had the previous year. 'We won't let our egos get in the way of the contestants,' said Simon, while Louis added, 'The slate has been wiped clean and we are starting anew.'

Sharon was also very much in agreement saying, 'It's not about us, it's about them, the contestants, and that's where the focus should be. To see so many people come to the auditions who have a dream, you hope for a few you can make that dream come true.'

Highlights – or rather lowlights – from the Series Two auditions included Total Eclipse, a duo from Wales who sing 'Summer of '69'. They're less than thrilled when Simon likens Fiona to Vicky Pollard from *Little Britain*, and calls her singing partner Pam 'A stretched version of her'.

Fiona is horrified and asks, 'So I look like a man?'. 'You don't look like a man,' exclaims Simon, about to make things a whole lot worse, 'You look like a man dressed as a woman.' 'So I look like a drag queen?' she responds. Erm, time to leave the room, ladies...

Eighty-three-year-old Dorothy Morrison is determined to have her time in the spotlight, and when she walks into the judges' room with her shopping trolley she immediately makes her feelings for Simon known and excitedly declares, 'At last, my hero!' Simon soon turns on the charm, telling her she's a 'saucy little thing' after she sings 'As Time Goes By'. And amazingly with three 'yes'es, she's through to bootcamp.

Fifty-nine-year-old supermarket cashier Beulah gets compared to Tina Turner and Shirley Bassey during her audition, but apparently that's not necessarily a good thing and doesn't guarantee her a place at bootcamp. Sadly she gets three 'no's, so it's back to scanning sausages for her. But it doesn't finish there. Louis defends her, jokingly saying that he was going to 'give her a chance', so Simon decides to hand her Louis' phone number. And just when everyone thinks he's given her a fake one, minutes later Louis answers his phone to discover that it's Beulah calling him from outside the hallway. 'I was just checking the number!' she trills happily.

Student Nicholas, 22, was convinced he had exactly what the judges were looking for. 'I am the best undiscovered talent in this country and when I sing Carlos Santana's "Smooth" I'm going to give it to you like you've never heard it sung before. Yeah baby, the real thing.'

But the judges don't exactly agree, with Louis telling him, 'I am speechless. With the great build-up I thought you were going to be a great singer but it wasn't very good.' After three 'no's Nicholas leaves the judges' room, but he can't help having the last word. 'Judges, you missed it!' he announces grandly.

But what have we here? Some good people? At last!

Glamour model Michelle Thorne is determined to prove that she's no dumb blonde and tells the judges, 'I'm not stupid, I play the piano, I play the guitar, I write my own songs – glamour girls aren't just tits, bums and blonde hair.'

After singing 'I Will Always Love You', she gets a 'no' from Louis but 'yes'es from Simon and Sharon, meaning she's through. 'I think she's really sweet and people will love her,' says Sharon.

Next there's Chico, who manages to charm everyone in the waiting room. But can he work his magic on the judges? Simon finds his performance loathsome and labels it, 'The corniest audition I've ever seen in my life.' It's a 'yes' from Sharon though, and despite Simon trying to convince him otherwise, Louis gives him the thumbs up, prompting Simon

to call an emergency (and rather angry) meeting with the show's producers.

Forty-one-year-old bin-man Andy does a great audition and it's a resounding 'yes' from all three who fall in love with his soulful voice, while 36-year-old Brenda gets pretty much the same treatment. She happened to be holidaying in the same hotel as the auditions were being held, so she decided to take her chances. She bounds into the room and gives a rousing performance. 'You do everything with gusto don't you?' Simon says to the bubbly lady. And with 'yes'es from Simon and Sharon, her risk has well and truly paid off.

The judges are also big fans of adorable MacKenzie, who sings Westlife's 'When You're Lookin' Like That'. But sadly, at just four years old, he's 12 years away from the minimum age. Damn those rules.

BOOTCAMP

OF THE 75,000 WHO AUDITIONED for Series Two, just 200 lucky acts remain. And by the time bootcamp is over, that number will have dwindled to just seven acts in each category. A thrilled Louis has been given the 16–24s to mentor, a happy Sharon's got the Over 25s, while a bewildered Simon has got the Groups.

The 16–24s head to North London's Arts Depot; Bingham Hall in Kent is the home to the Groups; while the Over 25s are hanging at London's hip Cafe De Paris club.

It's Day One at Louis' bootcamp and the hopefuls have to stand on the stage in groups of ten and sing one of five songs selected by him. A 20-year-old Manchester shop assistant called Shayne is the first to perform and gets a rousing reception, as does petit 16-year-old Trevor, who stunned the judges during his audition with his surprising booming voice. Meanwhile, Chenai is back for her second year, and is hoping that this year she'll make it past bootcamp; Louis

is feeling super-confident about his category saying, 'I'm convinced we've got the winner here.'

Over with Simon, things aren't going quite as brilliantly. He's worried about the standard of the groups and all-girl trio Addictiv Ladies leave him feeling less than impressed. Meanwhile, brothers Journey South have Simon pegged following their confusing audition: 'Simon just doesn't give anything away,' Andy muses.

The bonkers and the brilliant are on show at Sharon's bootcamp, from cross-dressing farmer Justin to cheeky Chico – who both shocks and pleases Sharon when he rips open his shirt!

At the end of Day One, the 200 have been whittled down to just 21 in each category. And by the end of Day Two, just a third will remain.

While Louis and Sharon's contenders spend the night before Day Two working hard on their performances for the next day, Simon treats his Groups to, er, a big booze up! Is that sensible?!

Louis' lot are given a song to learn overnight and have just one chance to perform it. Mum-of-one Michelle didn't make it as far as bootcamp last year so she's determined to prove her worth, as is 16-year-old James, who Louis is 'worried won't deliver on the live shows'.

Meanwhile, Simon tells the Groups they must, 'Impress me. There's no excuses today. You've got good songs.' The Conway Sisters fail to make a good impression when they mess up the words during their performance, but Journey South's act even brings tears to Andy's eyes.

Nerves are getting the better of some of Sharon's Over 25s, and several are gutted when they get their words muddled. Maria Lawson has an added pressure due to the fact that she's getting married the next day, but manages to give a belting performance of 'I'm Gonna Make You Love Me', which certainly grabs Sharon and her team's attention.

After some serious consideration the judges deliver their verdicts to their prospective contestants. There are some shocks in store – and an awful lot of sad faces.

THE JUDGES' HOUSES

THINGS TAKE A GLAMOROUS TURN during the Judges' Houses section of Series Two. While Simon's Groups head to his holiday home in sunny Spain, Louis' 16–24s go to his gorgeous home town of Dublin, and Sharon's get to go to – wait for it – Hollywood!

The excitement is evident, but the acts are also feeling the pressure as in just two days' time, three from each category will be cut from the competition.

You can literally feel how much each and every one of the hopefuls want to make it through to the live shows – and hopefully walk off with an incredible £1-million record deal.

Ozzy is on hand to dish out kisses to Sharon's acts while they look around wide-eyed at her lavish £11-million abode. Newlywed Maria is the first to perform in Sharon's garden, in front of a selection of her neighbours, including supermodel Rachel Hunter. When it comes to Chico's turn, he leaves even the Hollywood glitterati stunned when he strips off and dances in a swimming pool while performing 'Livin' La Vida Loca'.

Everyone's feeling the heat back in Spain where some people are about to make their last ever *X Factor* performance. Boy band The Brothers are first up and admit that, 'The next ten minutes could determine our futures.'

4Tune have been trying to make it big for ten years, including a stint in Series

One, so knowing that this could be one of their last opportunities to get noticed weighs heavy on their minds as they harmonize through 'I Don't Want to Talk about It'.

In Louis' penthouse in Dublin, worried Chenai is left in tears because she suspects that she has messed up in front of her mentor. Shayne – who has been panicking all day – is relieved when his performance of 'The Air That I Breathe' goes without a hitch, while cute little James manages to make one of Louis' team, Faye, cry with his rendition of 'Lately'.

But who's done enough to make it through to the live shows stage? Nine people in total must leave, and as Louis and his team sum up, they contemplate who could win the competition for them.

Louis decides to sleep on it and deliver his verdict the next morning, and when he does it's bad news for Trevor, James and Alexandra. Meanwhile, Sharon settles down to tell Haifa, Joanne and Ritchie that they haven't made it, and Simon breaks the bad news to Eskimo Blonde, The Brothers and Fourth Base.

SERIES TWO

THE
LIVE
SHOWS

SERIES TWO GOT OFF TO A BANG and the excitement continued all the way through to the end. The live shows saw judges sob, Chico drench himself in water and coin the phrase 'It's Chico Time' and Louis nearly leave the show. And it also saw some very emotional goodbyes.

Addictiv Ladies became the first casualties when they were booted out in Week 1.

In Show 2 it looked like Sharon was going to refuse to cast her vote as she did in Series One, but in the end she had her say and 4Tune left. They were swiftly followed by Phillip Magee in Week 3, whose rendition of 'Johnny B. Goode' simply wasn't enough to keep him in.

When Louis had the deciding vote between two of his acts in Week 4 – Chenai and Nicholas – despite giving an amazing performance of 'Always on My Mind', it was goodbye Chenai. There was a huge shock for everyone in Week 5 when Maria went head to head with The Conway Sisters – and lost out after Louis cast the deciding vote! Sharon called his decision a 'travesty' and was less than happy.

By Week 6 there were just seven acts left in the competition, and The Conway Sisters stayed in by the skin of their teeth once again, after being pitted against

after he hit out at Sharon and Simon saying that they had 'humiliated him'. But there were sighs of relief all round when Louis was back the following week having made up with his fellow judges.

It was soon revealed that The Conway Sisters' time was up in Week 7 when Simon chose to save his former foe, Chico, over them. With the penultimate show looming and just five contestants remaining, competition was at its fiercest. But sadly Chico's time was up and his journey came to an end in Week 8.

When the semi-final arrived, Shayne, Brenda, Journey South and Andy Abraham were the lucky ones left. Once the votes had been counted, a relieved Andy was the first to hear that he was safe, followed by a thrilled Shayne. Brenda and Journey South remained – but only one could go through, and Andy fell to the floor as it was announced that Journey South had landed the last place in the final. There were tears from Sharon as she hugged a sad Brenda, and even Louis welled up as he watched her final performance.

Nicholas. The poor girls had to endure a nasty reaction from the audience, who made it very clear that they thought Nicholas should have stayed – as did Louis. Following the show, rumours started circulating that Louis had quit

THE GRAND FINAL

IN A TWIST ON SERIES ONE, three acts were in the Grand Final during the second series of *The X Factor* – Journey South, Shayne Ward and Andy Abraham – meaning that one lucky act from each category made it all the way to the end.

Journey South are first to perform, and, flanked by Christmas trees, they do a beautiful rendition of Elton John's 'Don't Let the Sun Go Down on Me'. 'Great song choice, really well performed, you deserve to be here,' Louis tells them. An emotional Andy admits, 'This has been the most amazing, amazing experience of our lives.'

Andy Abraham is up next singing 'When a Man Loves a Woman' in his soulful tones. 'That was outstanding. You nailed it,' Simon says; while Sharon tells him adoringly, 'You are the thing dreams are made of.'

Shayne makes his first appearance of the night singing Daniel Bedingfield's 'If You're Not the One'. 'By any standard outside of a show like this, that was, in my opinion, absolutely flawless,' says an incredibly impressed Simon. Meanwhile, Shayne's mentor Louis

tells him, 'I absolutely think that you're a real, real star.'

Each of the acts gets to perform two more tracks each – a Christmas song and then another hit of their choice – before the first act is eliminated. Journey South sing 'Happy Xmas (War is Over)' and 'Let It Be' by The Beatles, Andy goes for 'O Holy Night' and 'Me and Mrs. Jones', while Shayne plumps for 'When a Child Is Born' and 'Over the Rainbow'.

Once all the songs have been sung and the votes have been counted, it's time to say goodbye to Journey South. The lads are clearly gutted but they take it in their stride and hug Andy and Shayne to say congratulations. Andy admits, 'I'm pretty gutted really. We wanted to win, but still, this has been the best ride of our lives and we want to thank everyone who has kept us here and got us this far.'

It's time for Andy and Shayne to go head to head in the Grand Final, and both attempt to win viewers' votes when they sing the winner's song, 'That's My Goal'.

Andy's up first and afterwards Louis tells him, 'You're an absolutely great guy and that was a great performance.'

Shayne takes to the stage for his turn and Simon – for the first time talking completely impartially having lost his own act, tells him – 'I think this competition has genuinely found a star, and in my opinion you have *The X Factor*.'

After one final performance it's time to discover who has triumphed in *The X Factor* 2005. And once the votes are counted, it's announced that the winner is... Shayne! And gracious Andy is the first to hug him and tell him well done.

In the audience, Shayne's friends, family and girlfriend Faye jump for joy, scream and cry. And it's not long before Shayne himself is crying and saying, 'I can't believe it!'

Shayne gets to watch as Andy Peters, holed up in a CD pressing plant, presses the button to start printing his debut single. And to round off the show he sings that very song, 'That's My Goal', to a thrilled audience as his proud former finalists join him on stage.

Addictiv Ladies

Fleur East, Nicola Owusu-Akontoh,
Vivienne Umeh, Stephanie Yamson

From: London

Auditioned: London

Mentor: Simon / Groups

Audition song: Missing You

Judge's house song: Wishing on a Star

Song sung at each stage of final:
1 Superstar

Final position: 12th

'I think you're brilliant,
I love you.' SHARON

The four members of Addictiv Ladies
– Stephanie, 17, Vivienne, 17, Fleur, 17, and
Nicola, 16 – met and became friends while
they were still in nursery school. They had
always sung together at a local drama and
song youth centre, and decided to become a
band for real three years before they entered
for *The X Factor*. The show wasn't their first
brush with fame, as they had previously sung
at Choice FM's 291 at the Hackney Empire.
They also performed at the Youth World
2003 and made it to the finals of the Essex
Star Search. They spent much of their time
performing at charity events, mainly at the
YMCA in their native Walthamstow.

All four girls were studying for their A-
Levels prior to their appearance on the show,
and worked part time at ELYA, an after-school
boys club teaching English and Maths. Mentor
Simon was a big fan of the ladies, but sadly
it seemed that Sharon and Louis weren't so
keen and they voted to save Chico over them,
prompting Simon Cowell to call Louis 'a
joke'. But the girls took it in their stride, with
Stephanie saying, 'It hurts, but we've made it
here. Half the people didn't!'

4Tune

Anthony Hannides, Mike Hannides, Philip Kemish and Simon Vitsaides

From: Southampton

Auditioned: London

Mentor: Simon / Groups

Audition song: Unchained Melody

Judge's house song: I Don't Want to Talk about It

Songs sung at each stage of final:
1 I Want It That Way
2 I'll Be There

Final position: 11th

4Tune are brothers Anthony, 18, and Mike, 21, their cousin Simon, 22, and Philip, 21, who Mike has been best mates with since secondary school. It was Mike and Phil who started the band when they were 13 after finding themselves performing in their school choir together. They later recruited Simon and Anthony and, calling themselves Four of a Kind, they used to get together at each others' houses and sing covers of tracks by artists like Backstreet Boys, Boyz II Men and Michael Jackson. They soon felt confident enough to showcase their talents to the world (well, their school) and won the annual talent competition (the same one which a certain Craig David – who also attended their school – had lost several years before).

They went on to win an MTV Base Lounge Open Mic Competition in 2004, and were awarded a Prince's Trust loan of £4,000 to help them build their own recording studio. Prior to the contest they were gigging at clubs and parties, writing songs, recording tracks and running live events for charity.

Despite appearances in Series One and Two and several knockbacks since, you can't keep a good band down, and the lads are currently working on their debut album.

'To have a group like you in a competition like this makes it that much more exciting.'
SIMON

'We've got something very special here.' LOUIS

Phillip Magee

Phillip has always been passionate about music, and at the tender age of four he used to wake up his whole house by putting music on so he could sing along loudly to it. His earliest influences were his mum – who was in a country music band and inspired him to sing – and Elvis Presley, who he remains a massive fan of to this day. He is also hugely keen on U2 and Bon Jovi.

He has always been musical, playing the piano at school, and started to teach himself guitar around seven years before he auditioned for *The X Factor*. He enjoyed showcasing his talents, and once won £100 in a karaoke competition which he admitted was slightly different to entering *The X Factor*!

Since *X Factor* Phillip has been kept busy with gigs across the UK, appeared on the TV show *Airline* and also took part in the Comic Relief launch alongside Chris Evans, David Walliams and Matt Lucas. He is still working hard on his music and plans to release a single later this year, about which he says, 'I've got a funny feeling that it's going to go a long way.'

Age: 21

From: Belfast

Auditioned: Belfast

Mentor: Louis / 16–24s

Audition song: Your Cheatin' Heart

Judge's house song: Don't Forget to Remember Me

Songs sung at each stage of final:
1 Amazed
2 Wind beneath My Wings
3 Johnny B. Goode

Final position: 10th

Chenai Zinyuku

Age: 19

From: Bradford

Auditioned: Manchester

Mentor: Louis / 16–24s

Audition song: Wish Upon a Star

Judge's house song: I'm Still Waiting

Songs sung at each stage of final:
1 The Closest Thing to Crazy
2 Young Hearts Run Free
3 Hero
4 Always on My Mind

Final position: 9th

Chenai was no stranger to the competition when she turned up to the auditions in Series Two. She was loved by the judges in Series One, but sadly got knocked out during the bootcamp stage. However, she was back with a vengeance when Series Two rolled around and decided to try again after her gran said she had received messages from God telling Chenai to audition once more as her exit from last year's show was not the end of her *X Factor* journey.

Previous to *The X Factor* Chenai had worked as a bank clerk and studied law at university, but had always dreamed of a career in music. She was influenced by soul singers such as Betty Wright, Bill Withers and Gladys Knight, but more recently has been listening to the likes of Hard-fi and James Blunt. With some help from her dad, himself a producer and performer, she started gigging to build up her confidence, and had an acoustic set once a month at the top of London department store Harvey Nichols. She also entered singing competitions, including Urban Voice 2003 at Jongleurs, which she won. Following *The X Factor* she put her law degree on hold to carry on working on her music, and plays numerous gigs around the UK.

'You deserve your place on that stage.' LOUIS

'I think you're fantastic.'
LOUIS

Maria Lawson

Age: 30
From: London
Auditioned: London
Mentor: Sharon / Over 25s
Audition song: Stop
Judge's house song: Since You've Been Gone
Songs sung at each stage of final:
1 Emotions
2 The Way You Make Me Feel
3 Piece of My Heart
4 You're Beautiful
5 Brown Sugar
Final position: 8th

Maria officially began her singing career aged 13 when she would use fake ID to sneak into pubs and clubs to perform. She later joined two girl bands, Slow Me and X-Pre, but sadly nothing came of them. Maria was signed to Peer Music between 2002 and 2005, and directly before her success on *The X Factor* was in a band called Skye, which was managed by her husband Lawrence Garry.

She also did extensive backing vocal work, appearing on Gabrielle's massive hit singles 'Out of Reach', 'Don't Need the Sun to Shine to Make Me Smile' and on a live version of 'Rise'. She later auditioned for the first series of *The X Factor* and made it into Simon's Over 25s category, but failed to make it past bootcamp. In Series Two he admitted that he'd slipped up and told her, 'I'm glad you've come back, I made a mistake last year.'

Bootcamp was a double celebration for Maria in Series Two – not only did she get through to the judges' houses round, but she also got married the day after being told that she'd made it to the next stage. After she was voted off the show Maria signed a record deal with Sony BMG and went on to score a top 20 hit with her single 'Sleepwalking' and a Number 41 hit with her self-titled debut album.

Nicholas Dorsett

'I think you're going to be a big, big star.' LOUIS

Age: 18

From: London

Auditioned: London

Mentor: Louis / 16–24s

Audition song: End of the Road

Judge's house song: You Make Me Feel Brand New

Songs sung at each stage of final:
1 On the Wings of Love
2 Let's Get It On
3 Let's Stay Together
4 I Want You Back
5 I Believe I Can Fly
6 If I Ever Fall in Love

Final position: 7th

Nicholas started singing along to records when he was just three, but it was only at 14 that he decided to take things to another level and began entering talent competitions, including one for Choice FM which he won. This led to him landing a place in a boy band, but he quit when he decided that the manager who had been assigned to the band wasn't giving it his all.

He continued gigging in his local area to get his name known and improve his confidence, and had just reached the final of an unsigned acts competition when he reached the latter stages of *The X Factor*. After being voted off *The X Factor* in the fifth week, he bowed out gracefully and said, 'I can't say I didn't deserve to go because everyone in that competition was very talented... I'm just happy that I was able to do it and I feel really grateful.'

He stuck with his music and performed across the UK on *The X Factor* tour alongside his fellow competitors. In March 2007 he won the UK Unsigned Best and Most Successful Contestant at the UK Unsigned Awards, and is currently in the process of writing and recording new material in the hope of landing a record deal.

The Conway Sisters

Sisters Sharon, 28, Sinead, 23, Marie, 21 and Laura, 18 come from a musical background and started singing together at a young age. They began performing as a professional band three years before entering *The X Factor*, and managed themselves with the help of their dad.

Sharon and Laura write most of the songs for the band, and through hard work and determination the foursome managed to rack up two top twenty hits and one top ten hit in their native Ireland, despite not having a record deal. They promoted the singles by performing in shopping centres and car parks, while their dad controls the production, distribution and marketing of the tracks.

Shortly before auditioning for *The X Factor* they began on their debut album in London with Simon Hill, who has also worked with the likes of Kylie, Natasha Bedingfield and Natalie Imbruglia. The girls had also supported Westlife on tour and appeared at their homecoming gig, which boasted an audience of 20,000. In fact, Shane from Westlife was so impressed with their act that he invited them to sing at his wedding in December 2003.

The sisters released their debut album following their exit from the show, and were nominated for Best Irish Pop Act in the 2006 Meteor Ireland Music Awards. However, they split in 2006 saying, 'We will be finishing up as The Conway Sisters for now; we've come to a place where we want to pursue individual career paths and now we feel ready to do that! For the record there have been no fall-outs or fights, it's all been very amicable and as sisters we're closer now than ever.' Laura is now pursuing a solo career.

> 'I think it was a good performance. A strong performance.'
> **SIMON**

Laura Conway, Marie Conway, Sharon Conway, Sinead Conway

From: Sligo

Auditioned: Belfast

Mentor: Simon / Groups

Audition song: In Your Eyes

Judge's house song: You Raise Me Up

Songs sung at each stage of final:
1 S.O.S.
2 You Raise Me Up
3 Total Eclipse of the Heart
4 One Voice
5 Hold On
6 One Moment in Time
7 Nothing's Gonna Stop Us Now

Final position: 6th

'We love you.'
SHARON

Chico Slimani

There were mixed reactions to former goat herder Chico when he auditioned for *The X Factor*, with Simon leaving the judges' room in disgust when he was put through. But Chico didn't let that dent his confidence and he described himself as 'Talented with a capital "t", Fun with a capital "f" and Charismatic with a capital "c".' He was born in Wales and later moved to Morocco when his parents split up, but came back to the UK when he was 14. He has a City and Guilds in Mechanical Engineering and has worked as a hairdresser, electrician and stripper, as well as dabbling in film and music. He has also toured the UK and Ibiza after singing on the StuntMaster club track 'The Ladyboy Is Mine' in 2001.

After he was voted out, Chico released two singles – the Number 5 hit 'It's Chico Time' (a phrase which was coined during the live shows) and the follow-up, a cover of Ottawan's 'D.I.S.C.O.' which got to Number 25. In June 2006 he and his girlfriend had a baby, Lalla-Khira, about whom he said, 'She's a healthy, happy, bouncing bundle of joy and I'm really enjoying bringing her up.'

As well as touring extensively, he's also involved with a production company called Unity Films and has started a charity called The Rainbow Child Foundation which helps raise money for children around the world.

Age: 34

From: London

Auditioned: London

Mentor: Sharon / Over 25s

Audition songs: If You Ever; Kiss

Judge's house song: Livin' La Vida Loca

Songs sung at each stage of final:
1 Da Ya Think I'm Sexy
2 Play That Funky Music
3 Livin' La Vida Loca
4 Kiss
5 Hero
6 It's Chico Time
7 Billie Jean
8 I Got You (I Feel Good); Time Warp

Final position: 5th

63

Bubbly Brenda entered *The X Factor* completely by chance when she found herself staying in the same hotel as the auditions were taking place during a romantic weekend away with her husband Patrick. But while the romance went slightly out the window when Brenda spent most of the time queuing to be seen by the judges, Patrick was there every step of the way and was every bit as thrilled as she was when she was put through to the bootcamp rounds. 'I had no proper make-up and absolutely nothing to wear!' she laughs, remembering her panicked performance.

Brenda's early life was marred with tragedy when her parents were killed in a car crash when she was just a young girl. She and her brother Rodney were raised by their grandmother, aunts and uncles, and it was at her local Pentecostal church where Brenda's grandmother was 'The Mother' (vicar) that she developed her love for singing while performing in the Sunday school junior choir. Brenda later became the choir mistress and sang for the Pentecostal collective Church Of God In Christ (C.O.G.I.C.) mass choir. She soon realised that music was to play a huge part in her life, and aged 18 she began singing in local clubs and at parties in the

Age: 36

From: London

Auditioned: Belfast

Mentor: Sharon / Over 25s

Audition song: River Deep, Mountain High

Judge's house song: I Just Want to Make Love to You

Songs sung at each stage of final:
1 Son of a Preacher Man
2 Rescue Me
3 Midnight Train to Georgia
4 Somebody Else's Guy
5 Heartbreaker
6 Last Dance
7 I Will Always Love You
8 I'm Outta Love; I'll Never Love This Way Again
9 Respect; Without You

Final position: 4th

Brenda Edwards

'You owned the
stage tonight.' LOUIS

'Very, very good
indeed.' SIMON

hope that she would get spotted by an
eagle-eyed talent scout. The next few years
were spent attending auditions, sending off
demos and hoping that she would get her
break. She had some success in 1989 when
she sang at the Hackney Empire in the
semi-final of Channel 4's 291 competition.
She also worked as a session singer, and
reached Number 12 in the UK club charts
when she sang for Mr. Jack on his track
'Wiggly World Part 2'.

Whilst waiting for her break she took a
job in an accounts office to support her two
children, Jamal and Tanisha. She stayed
in the job for 17 years while continuing to
perform for friends and family at parties
and weddings.

All Brenda's hard work has now paid
off as she finally got the recognition she
dreamed of and deserved. She now makes
a living full-time from her music and is
writing and recording her own songs.
She also enjoyed a long stint in the well-
respected West End show *Chicago* playing
Mama Morton and in the spring of 2007
she performed sold-out gigs at London's
hip Pigalle club and the legendary Ronnie
Scott's jazz club.

Journey South

Andy Pemberton and Carl Pemberton

From: Middlesbrough

Auditioned: Birmingham

Mentor: Simon / Groups

Audition song: I Still Haven't Found What I'm Looking For

Judge's house song: Desperado

Songs sung at each stage of final:
1 Something about the Way You Look Tonight
2 Desperado
3 Angel of Harlem
4 The First Time Ever I Saw Your Face
5 Livin' on a Prayer
6 Angels
7 I Still Haven't Found What I'm Looking For
8 Bad Day; Candle in the Wind
9 Let It Be; You're in My Heart
Final: Don't Let the Sun Go Down on Me; Happy Christmas (War Is Over); Let It Be

Final position: 3rd

'I give you a good song and you perform it one hundred per cent.'
SIMON

'You guys appeal to everyone.'
SHARON

Brothers Andy and Carl formed a band after Andy watched his brother touring the clubs and bars of their native Middlesbrough and decided that he wanted a piece of the action. They enlisted a drummer, bass player and keyboard player and the band began gigging together around the North-east, calling themselves The Answer.

They also entered a number of battle-of-the-bands-style competitions and it was while they were taking part in one in Romford that a manager spotted them and suggested that they moved down to London to try their luck. So five years ago Carl gave up his plumbing apprenticeship three months before completing it, bought a caravan on a credit card and the band moved to the big smoke. This was when the name Journey South was born, summing up what the lads were doing.

The band lived in a caravan for two years gigging at open mic nights and writing songs. The three band members left and were replaced by local musicians, and in 2001 they did a showcase to potential record companies. However, nothing came of it, and after splitting with their manager, money troubles meant that they had to head home after realising that they were a whopping £20,000 in debt.

They went back to everyday jobs working for a commercial property company but continued performing at weddings and parties, never giving up hope that their break would come. And in 2005, it did – in the shape of *The X Factor* auditions.

The duo were an instant hit with the judges and they felt like finally this could be their big moment. They weren't wrong: despite losing out to Andy and Shayne in the final, the band were reported to have been offered an impressive five record contracts following the show, and eventually signed with Simon Cowell to Sony BMG.

They released their self-titled debut album in April 2006, which went straight to Number 1 and sold 216,000 copies in its first week. It went on to become the sixth best-selling album of 2006, shifting an amazing 600,000 copies and has now been certified double platinum. Carl and Andy have also appeared on numerous TV shows, toured extensively around the UK, and in August 2006 they were invited to The Prince's Trust Garden Party as a thank you for all the support they had given to the charity. They were stunned when Prince Charles remembered them from a meeting five months earlier, and even lent them his private jet so they could fly between their gigs in London and Scotland. They are currently dividing their time between Sweden and the UK while they work on their second album.

Andy Abraham

'You are smooth, you're soulful, you're sensual.'
LOUIS

Age: 40

From: London

Auditioned: London

Mentor: Sharon / Over 25s

Audition song: A Song for You

Judge's house song: My Cherie Amour

Songs sung at each stage of final:
1 Greatest Love of All
2 You to Me are Everything
3 Unforgettable
4 Can't Take My Eyes Off You
5 I'll Make Love to You
6 Me and Mrs. Jones
7 I Have Nothing
8 Easy Lover; When I Fall in Love
9 (Everything I Do) I Do It For You; Lately
Final: When a Man Loves a Woman; O Holy
Night; Me and Mrs. Jones; That's My Goal

Final position: 2nd

'Mrs O is very proud of you, Andy.' SHARON

Andy discovered his natural ability for singing from a young age, but it wasn't until some years later that he decided to showcase his talents for a wider audience than family and friends.

Despite his sister pushing him throughout his teens to take up singing professionally, it wasn't until his 20s that he took her advice and tried his luck on the local singing circuit near his London home. He began going to the 291 Club at the Hackney Empire and the audience instantly loved him. With his confidence growing he went on to take part in a competition at the Brixton Academy.

When his best friend died of heart disease in 1998, the tragic event made Andy realise that life is short and you have to follow your dreams. He quit his day job as a printer and went to the Powerhouse music college in Acton to hone his talents. He formed an R'n'B/pop band called True Mix with some fellow students and together they wrote over 30 songs.

After leaving college he continued as a session singer – something which he had always done. While working for London transport, he entered the TV show *This Is My Moment*, and came a very respectable second. He later became a bin-man, but then his wife, Denise, decided to enter him for a certain TV show, forging his signature on the application form in the process. But it wasn't an opportunity Andy was about to miss.

When his *X Factor* audition rolled around, the judges – and in particular Sharon – became instant fans. He was stunned when he made it through to bootcamp, then sailed through the judges' houses round, and eventually found himself on the live shows.

Andy may have narrowly missed winning *The X Factor*, but thanks to his incredible soulful voice and loveable demeanour he built up a huge fan base. When the show came to an end he was offered a deal with Management Company Global Talent, and a record deal with Sony BMG.

After years of struggling, the title of his debut album – *The Impossible Dream* – seemed incredibly fitting. It reached Number 1 in the UK upon its March 2006 release, and also went to Number 2 in the Republic of Ireland. The follow-up, November 2006's 'Soul Man', reached Number 19 in the UK. Andy was undoubtedly one of the nicest contestants *The X Factor* has ever had. He is continuing to perform at gigs around the UK, and is currently working on new music.

'Look at you, you're gorgeous!' SHAR

Shayne Ward

'Shayne, you have it all.'
LOUIS

Manchester lad Shayne Ward stood out to *X Factor* viewers from the moment he walked into the judges' audition room. Dressed casually in jeans and a hooded top, he wowed the judges with his rendition of Elton John's 'Sacrifice' and was soon through to the next round. Just a matter of months later he celebrated his first Number 1 with 'That's My Goal' – and he's never looked back.

Prior to trying out for *The X Factor* Shayne was working in the shoe section of a clothes shop and was also in a band called Destiny alongside two friends, Tracy Murphy and Tracey Lyle. Despite having already entered *Popstars: The Rivals* and made it to the top thirty in 2002, it was his sisters who encouraged him to give *The X Factor* a go, and they even called up to get an application form for him.

Nearly eleven million votes were cast in the Grand Final, and Shayne pipped his closest rival Andy Abraham at the post. He was soon being chauffeured around and being interviewed left, right and centre while awaiting the release of his debut single. 'That's My Goal' sold an incredible 313,000 copies on its first day of release, making it the fourth fastest-selling single of all time.

He released his follow up song, 'No Promises', on 10 April 2006. It went in at Number 2 and was swiftly followed by his debut, self-titled album, which hit shops on 17 April and went straight to Number 1 after selling 201,266 copies in the first week alone.

Shayne's third single, 'Stand by Me', released in July 2006, went to Number 17 in the UK and Number 9 in Ireland. Meanwhile, the rest of the world were also being introduced to Shayne's many talents, with success coming in numerous other countries, including South Africa and Taiwan.

Disaster struck though in August 2006 when Shayne discovered that he had developed vocal chord nodules and he was immediately flown to the US where he received emergency treatment. Thankfully the surgery was successful and he was soon back in the studio working on his follow-up album, and in early 2007 he embarked on a tour around the UK and Ireland, playing 18 dates.

The first single from his second album, 'If That's Okay with You', was released on 24 September and provided Shayne with yet another hit!

Age: 20

From: Manchester

Auditioned: Manchester

Mentor: Louis / 16–24s

Audition song: Sacrifice

Judge's house song: The Air That I Breathe

Songs sung at each stage of final:
1 Right Here Waiting
2 If You're Not the One
3 Summer of '69
4 You Make Me Feel Brand New
5 Cry Me a River
6 A Million Love Songs
7 I Believe in a Thing Called Love
8 Take Your Mama; Careless Whisper
9 If Tomorrow Never Comes; Unchained Melody
Final – If You're Not the One; When a Child Is Born; Over the Rainbow; That's My Goal

Final position: 1st

INTERVIEW WITH SHAYNE

What made you decide to enter for the show?
My sisters went for it, and they persuaded me to. I said no at first, but they phoned up for an application form for me, so I filled it in and the rest was history. I owe them a lot!

You were already singing though?
Yes, I was already in a band at the time, Destiny, and I was really happy doing gigs at the weekend and stuff and I was very proud of it. I didn't expect anything big to come out of my singing which is why I never went in for competitions.

Were you nervous in your audition?
The auditions were really weird because I missed my first one because I was away on holiday. But luckily enough when I got back there was an open day so I went along. I remember walking into the room and the nerves left my body and I felt really focused, which is something that's very rare when people get in front of those judges!

Most people panic more when they walk into the audition room...
I know, and I still don't know to this day why it happened. I just thought 'I've got something to do here. I've got to sing in front of these three important people and I'm going to sing my heart out'.

How did you feel the moment it was announced that you'd won *The X Factor*?
All I could do was scream! I could hear the crowd and all these things were going through my head. I remember shouting over to Andy because I thought he was going to win, and when they said my name it was one of the most amazing feelings in the world.

How has your life changed since winning *The X Factor*?
It's changed for the better. Doing something I love for a living is incredible. Just being able to travel the world and sing to thousands of people and have them sing back to you is an incredible

thing. I've come a long way and achieved so much, it's incredible. I'm being honoured into the Variety Club in Manchester, and the last person to get that was Shirley Bassey, which feels amazing.

Have you got used to being recognised?
Well, you have to learn to adapt very quickly because it's a life-changing thing. I was kind of prepared for it at first, but it's still very strange. I like people recognising me though, because at the end of the day it's the public that put me here. So I like signing autographs and having photos taken.

Who have you kept in touch with from the show?
Andy, Brenda, Chico and a lot of the crew. We had a great team.

Would you recommend other people to go on *The X Factor*?
Definitely, one hundred per cent. People can be trying a lifetime to get into the music industry because it's so hard to get into, and being on the show gives you a huge opportunity.

73

How were *The X Factor* auditions for you?
The first day was a bit ropey, but it always is! Thankfully things got better.

Did you have any loons?
Of course! We had one lady who said she was doing it for her dead horse, then her grandmother who was having a hip replacement, and then herself. She wanted to be a success for them all. She said that if she won she would invite us over to Cancun in Mexico because she's going to build a holiday home there.

Well that's your next holiday sorted...
Done and dusted!

What's been your favourite category?
In the past it's been the young ones, but the Groups have been really good. I want to find the next Spice Girls. We need a nice fun pop act.

What's been your worst audition moment of all time?
There was this guy who came during the second series and he looked like Guy Fawkes and absolutely stank. Even from ten foot away he smelt so bad it made me feel sick. I know people use the term 'I'm going to throw up' lightly, but I honestly thought I was going to.

What's been your funniest audition moment ever?
I think the Spanish lady, Penelope. She was so lovely and she laughed at herself in the end. She laughed at us laughing at her. She had such a good spirit about her. She was just such great fun.

Who have been the most spine-tingling singers you've had?
Andy Abraham, Shayne and Leona. They were all 'goose-bump' moments. You just got that feeling when they sang... Andy got me with 'Me and Mrs. Jones', and Shayne singing 'Over the Rainbow' in the final just was an unbelievable performance.

Are there any songs you hate to hear when people audition?
I can't stand hearing people do 'Hero' by

Mariah Carey or 'Beautiful' by Christina Aguilera. They're impossible songs to better. Or anything by Whitney Houston. They're three of the best female singers of all time so you can't take a song like that and better it. Just stop!

Is there anything that makes you instantly think 'no' when someone walks into the room?
You can honestly tell by somebody's demeanour when they walk in. Obviously you take into consideration nerves and things. Some people are shy. Leona was very shy initially, but she still had an aura about her. But some people walk in and they're either aggressive, or you know before they even start that it's a road to nowhere.

Be honest – do you ever put people through just because you like them?
I do, and I put them through to a certain stage. You give them the benefit of the

doubt and you hope that the next time you see them they'll take it up a notch, and if they don't, you have to let them go. And you know, if you know they may not be right but you'll make their year, then why not? Where's the harm?

Who are you proudest to have mentored?
Andy. He's a great guy with a great family. They're all-round good people and you wish them so much luck.

Are there any contestants that you think got away and you wish you'd picked?
No, I don't think we've had any Jennifer Hudson moments on this show. No one that got away. Sure, every time there's a winner you think 'I wish I had that one', but I think I've been lucky with who I had. And this will be my year!

Who do you wish you'd mentored most out of all the hopefuls?
Penelope could have done a lot of comedy because she genuinely didn't know what she did was hysterical! I was very proud of Brenda. She was a great entertainer. It's not about having hit records because there are so many different roads to make it in entertainment, and she always belonged in theatre and she made it in *Chicago*. She's got a real spark and she was like the ugly duckling who turned into a swan at the end. It was amazing to see.

Are you still in touch with many of the contestants?
I'm very much in touch with Andy and his family. They're wonderful.

Are you excited about Dannii coming on board?
Very excited, but it's exciting to try something new. And Dannii's a little firecracker. There's no floss on her.

Will you and Simon be enjoying some of your usual arguments during this series?
I just ignore him now! I'm like 'don't even go there'. But I enjoy the banter. I can take him on though.

What are you most looking forward to about this series?
This series is kind of going into the unknown. There are a lot of different twists with this series and new people on the panel. I'm looking forward to the changes.

SERIES THREE

THE EARLY STAGES

*T*HE X FACTOR AUDITIONS have become famous for attracting the weird and the wonderful to its doors in search of fame. And the auditions for the third series definitely didn't disappoint.

The very first auditionee in Manchester was a landscape gardener called Tim, who admitted that he'd spent the last six months perfecting his routine. But his practice failed to pay off with Simon telling him, 'I've got absolutely no idea why you had any encouragement whatsoever. It is about as bad as it can possibly get.'

Sadly Tim kind of set the tone for the entire day, and the judges found the Manchester auditions a touch disappointing. It looked like it was going to be a similar story in London, judging by the first person to try their luck.

Donna's dream was to be as successful as Madonna, but her slightly terrifying rendition of her idol's hit 'Like a Prayer' leaves the judges open-mouthed.

But thankfully things are soon looking up and our regular threesome – who are joined by *American Idol* judge and former pop star Paula Abdul who makes a surprise appearance – soon see some acts with real potential.

Sisters Karen, Claudia and Natasha, a.k.a. Pure Liberty, were the first group to be put through to bootcamp and caused Paula to exclaim, 'I adore you guys; you're so much fun and so talented.'

A certain Leona Lewis soon made an appearance and was told in a rare moment of joy by Simon that she was 'Absolutely fantastic' and did 'a great audition'.

Six-piece harmony group The Unconventionals also make the grade, as again Simon almost cracks a smile as he tells them, 'We could bottle you lot and

sell you because you have made every single person in this room smile.'

But after such a good run, there just had to be another shocker around the corner, and it came in the form of Michael Jackson fan Onkar. After displaying singing skills so bad you fear he would make your ears bleed, the 31-year-old was told in no uncertain terms by the judges that he was one of the worst auditions they'd ever had. But he wasn't about to leave the room without having his say and told them, 'Don't judge the judge please, because there is only one judge, and that's me, Onkar Judge.' Righty-ho.

And there's worse to come for Simon when choir singer Lorraine's 86-year-old mother-in-law takes offence at Simon's cruel comments towards her and tells him, 'You laughed, you need to alter your ways Simon... You think you're better than everyone, but I think you are ignorant. Yes, you were very ignorant Simon'.

For perhaps the first time in his life Simon is virtually speechless, just managing to mutter a couple of 'sorry's before later admitting, 'I have never been so humiliated in my life.'

Thankfully things are soon looking up and Bristol spawns the handsome Ashley, who leaves the judges smiling from ear to ear. As does aspiring opera singer Paris who prompts Sharon to tell her she's 'a breath of fresh air'. But there's disappointment when the Liverpool lass admits that she's only 14, and therefore two years too young to enter the competition. Ah well, only a couple more years to wait...

There's some comfort in the form of an 18-year-old called Raymond, whose rendition of Dean Martin's 'Ain't That a Kick in the Head' leaves all the judges filled with hope.

But would you believe it? There are also a few who are not so good... Student Warren shocks them with a bizarre dance

routine, which includes him doing the splits, and he ends up being escorted from the room after calling Simon a 'panto queen'. Meanwhile, 57-year-old David fails to impress with his slightly creepy performance of 'Sexy Lady'.

Next it's on to Birmingham where boy band 4Sure impress the judges when they harmonize on Daniel Bedingfield's 'If You're Not the One' and instantly secure their place at bootcamp.

But is the news going to be as good for 17-year-old Kylie? She confidently claims, 'I am Kylie, but you can call me K Star. K is for Kylie and Star, because I am a star. This isn't a dream it's a reality, and I will be having a Number One single and a massive-selling album.' Sadly, her dreams are shattered when Simon tells her, 'The truth – you'll never make a career in music. It's hard when you're good but it is impossible when you are just OK.' Kylie's mum soon storms into the room to confront Simon, but he is unrepentant and tells her, 'You are giving your daughter false hope, you have led her down the wrong path, she will never be a pop star.'

Thankfully there's more love in the room when 24-year-old Vicky auditions and reveals that she is Louis' biggest fan. 'I've got a fan site for you and everything,' she says before admitting that it's only got, erm, 45 members...

BOOTCAMP

ONE HUNDRED AND EIGHTY aspiring *X Factor* contestants were chosen from the nationwide auditions during Series Three, but with only 21 people going through to the next round, the pressure was on when it was time to head to bootcamp.

All the judges took some experts along to help them with the tough decision-making process. Louis' took place at the Broadway Theatre in Essex where he was accompanied by Westlife's Kian Egan and vocal coach Yvie Burnett. Sharon, record company exec Adrian Williams and vocal coach Mark Hudson headed to hip Soho nightclub Too2Much, while Simon went to the plush Avington Park country house in Winchester with singer Sinitta.

Things didn't get off to a great start on Day One, though, with Louis claiming of the Groups, 'I saw no star acts there, it is not looking good.'

Sharon was soon putting her foot down and sternly warned the Over 25s, 'You are all over twenty-five and you may never get this chance again. So impress me, do not waste it. Don't blow it guys, because you know what, I want to win this year!'

And never one to hold back, Simon told the 16–24s. 'You have to come in believing you can win. Most of you I have seen so far today have come in like you are half dead, and the bad news is that I am going to double up on the number of people I am sending home at the end of today as a consequence. I was going to keep more but after this morning I have changed my mind, so if you haven't got it you might as well go home.'

After some serious consideration as the first day came to an end, the 16–24s were cut from 81 to 30, the Groups from 32 groups to 16, and the Over 25s from 60 to 16 places.

Happily for the judges, things started to look up on Day Two. The acts, clearly knowing that they needed to pull their

socks up after the judges' harsh words,
stayed up late into the night practising in
a bid to impress them.

But no matter how far they'd come
on, not everyone could go through, and
it was time to say goodbye to some very
disappointed contestants. A mere seven
acts from each category were in with
a chance of going through to the next
round, so the judges had to be ruthless
– something which doesn't come naturally
to all of them.

And in the end, it was the man who is
considered to be the world's toughest-
talking judge who found the cull most
difficult, and eventually managed to
convince the producers to let him put
through eight acts instead of seven.

A total of 22 acts got the opportunity
to go to the judges' houses where they
prayed that they would shine sufficiently
to make it onto the coveted live show.
But not everyone can be a winner...

THE JUDGES' HOUSES

WITH 22 ACTS DESPERATE for a place in the live shows, once again the judges and their trusty experts headed off to the places where they feel most comfortable to make the tough decisions. Simon headed to an incredible house in Miami to lap up the sun with his contestants, Sharon went to the Dorchester Hotel in London, where she is a regular guest, while Louis' finalists got to stay at Ireland's beautiful Dromoland Castle.

After the friendly banter of auditions, the judges' competitive streaks start to emerge with Louis claiming, 'I want to win the competition again this year and I think with the eight acts I have, as long as they raise their game, I think I could do it.'

Sharon is nervous about whittling her eight Over 25s down to four, and has quite a job on her hands. The likes of Ben Mills, Jonathan Bremner, Katie Agnus and 62-year-old OAP Lyn Fairbanks are all brilliant in their own way and Sharon admits that she loves them all, so it's not going to be easy.

It's a family affair for Louis in the Groups category where both The Brothers and The MacDonald Brothers are desperate to be chosen, while three-piece girl band Dolly Rockers want to do it for the ladies, with Lucy saying, 'We are the only girl group left and although we know we are not the strongest act here we have improved so much and we really want to make Louis proud.'

rants, 'What is going on with you today? Your language and attitude is all wrong, you've walked in like a loser.'

And as he's up against brilliant acts like Leona Lewis, Nikitta Angus, Shaun Rogerson and Ray Quinn, annoying Simon probably isn't the best idea.

The judges have some tough choices to make, and whatever they decide there is destined to be tears of both joy and sadness. And there are lots and lots of them...

Louis also has his fair share of boy bands, including 4Sure, Eton Road and Avenue who reckon they have the potential to set the charts on fire. Band member Jamie says, 'There are not many boy bands in the charts at the moment and we want to rectify that and we think we have something really different to offer.'

Not surprisingly, things don't go exactly smoothly with Simon's selection when he has a showdown with one contestant before he's even started. Twenty-year-old Ashley Mackenzie is less than happy with the song Simon has chosen for him to perform – the George Michael track 'I Can't Make You Love Me' – while Simon is livid that he's moaning despite the incredible opportunity he's been presented with. He soon takes him aside to tell him in no uncertain terms and

SERIES THREE

THE LIVE SHOWS

WITH 12 ACTS VYING for a place in the final, the tension was evident from the very first live show of Series Three. Having seen how well the previous year's winner, Shayne, had done, all the contestants were keen to emulate his success.

Week 1 saw Lionel Ritchie pop by and Simon and Louis have their first argument of the all-live extravaganzas! The Unconventionals became the first act to go with Simon telling them, 'I loved you in your first audition, but tonight you were diabolical.'

Rod Stewart graced the stage in Week 2 and Simon and Louis traded insults about each other. But Simon had the last laugh when the second of Louis' acts, boy band 4Sure, were sent home.

Week 3 saw legend Tony Bennett perform and brought about a shock twist when two of Sharon's acts – Dionne and Kerry – were voted off the competition.

Week 4 was Abba week, and Bjorn Ulvaeus was on hand to give advice to the aspiring singers. But having been saved last week, it was Ashley's turn to say his goodbyes, making him the first of Simon's acts to go. Simon was, needless to say, not very happy and lashed out at Louis calling him 'spiteful' for voting Ashley off.

A genuine smoothie appeared on Show 5 – the incredible Julio Iglesias. There

were just seven acts left, and when the bottom two were announced, Simon was shocked to discover that they were Ray and Nikitta, who were both his acts. And it was Ray who stayed safe while Nikitta sang for the last time.

Westlife and Delta Goodrem appeared in Show 6. All the judges were down to an equal two acts each with just one girl remaining, the lovely Leona. But Louis soon lost another of his contestants in Robert.

Housewives' favourites Il Divo were Week 7's special guests as all the acts belted out tracks from classic films. Eton Road and Ben Mills polled lowest, and Simon chose to send Eton Road home,

much to Louis' disgust. And Louis was equally as unhappy in Week 8 when his final act, The MacDonald Brothers, left after an amazing 3.5 million votes were cast. But hey, at least they got to meet the incredible Barry Manilow, who was the guest celebrity singer.

When the semi-final rolled around, Ray, Leona and Ben were joined by Gloria Estefan. The competition was incredibly close and it was anyone's guess as to which two acts would make it all the way to the final. Sharon had one act to Simon's two, and the smile on Simon's face was a mile wide when it was revealed that Ben was out, and Leona and Ray were to face each other in the Grand Final.

THE GRAND FINAL

OF THE 100,000 ACTS who applied for a place on Series Three of *The X Factor*, just two remained in the Grand Final – Simon's acts Leona Lewis and Raymond Quinn.

With a £1-million record deal up for grabs, the talented twosome were determined to give their all and show the public why they should walk away with the incredible prize on offer.

Tensions were high even before the live show began, with Leona and Ray promising to support each other as much as they could through the next nerve-wracking few hours. Ray said, 'Leona and I have come all the way through bootcamp and Miami, and I knew that she would go all the way and be in the final, but I never thought I would. To be able to share it with her is amazing, I feel so good about it.'

Meanwhile Leona said, 'We've got our work cut out for us but Ray and I are just going to go for it and hopefully it will be a great show.'

Every bit of hard work the pair had put in during the series had led up to this moment and the chance to release the beautiful ballad 'A Moment Like This' as their first single. A celeb-packed audience looked on as the duo took a thousand deep breaths, said silent prayers and sang like they've never sung before.

Ray crooned 'My Way' and 'Fly Me to the Moon' by Frank Sinatra, as well as a duet with Westlife on that other Frank favourite, 'That's Life'.

Meanwhile Leona belted out Whitney Houston's 'I Will Always Love You' and Celine Dion's version of 'All by Myself', and was joined on stage by Take That to sing the band's hit 'A Million Love Songs'.

Both also performed the winner's single, and then all they could do was sit back and wait for the votes to roll in and the result to be announced.

Both Leona and Ray had their fair share of celebrity supporters. Among Leona's fans were Ricky Gervais ('Leona is ridiculously good. America good') and Rod Stewart ('She did look good and has an incredible voice'); while fighting Ray's corner were Tony Bennett ('There's a certain thing – I call it the "it factor" – and as far as I'm concerned he's got it') and Abba's Bjorn Ulvaeus ('I think he stands a good chance – he exudes enthusiasm').

But there could only be one winner, and as Leona and Ray stood nervously hand in hand in the middle of the stage, it was announced that the winner of *The X Factor* 2007 was Leona.

After some tears and hugs from Ray, it was over to Andy Peters who was at the CD factory where the winner's single would be pressed, and Leona watched as her debut release was put into production. It was time for the final performance of the series – Leona singing 'A Moment Like This'. And for anyone watching, there was no doubting that her moment had well and truly arrived.

The Unconventionals

The Unconventionals were formed when singer Drew decided to create a group that sounded great, but didn't put too much emphasis on how the band members looked. He was keen for them to look different to conventional groups, hence the name.

Drew met Andrew while performing at a charity gig in 1990 and then got to know Liz when they played boyfriend and girlfriend in a stage show of *Grease*. Nicola and Lucy met Drew when they all worked on the Boy George musical *Taboo*. Tom, the sixth and final member of the band, is Nicola's boyfriend. The band had only been performing together for two months before applying for *The X Factor* and had just one gig under their belts – a charity performance at London club Too2Much.

However, each and every one of them had dreamed of finding fame in the music or theatre industries and saw *The X Factor* as the perfect launch pad. Drew admitted honestly, 'I've reached a point where my career is at a crossroads and not going so well, so this could bring a way of earning a decent living and doing what I love to do.'

The band are still working on music, touring and they supported Westlife in the spring of 2007.

'You're very good at what you do.' SHARON

Nicola Dawn, Liz Ewing, Drew Jaymson, Andrew Newey, Tom Newman, Lucy Newton

From: London

Auditioned: London

Mentor: Louis / Groups

Audition song: On Top of the World

Judge's house song: Dedicated to the One I Love

Song sung at each stage of final:
1 Dancing in the Street

Final position: 12th

4Sure – Andrew Fisher, 30, Kriss Jones, 24, Donovan Bailey, 38, and Jermaine Sanderson, 23 – were formed in 2003 by singer/songwriter/producer Donovan. Kriss sang down the phone to him and was instantly in, while friends Jermaine and Andrew joined around the same time.

They chose the name 4Sure because they were 'four guys sure of their destiny' and prior to auditioning for *The X Factor* they spent their time performing around the country at various pubs and holiday parks. They entered the competition to, in their words, 'raise their profile and secure a record deal'.

Before *The X Factor*, their biggest claims to fame had been singing with the band Take 6 at a workshop (Donovan) and meeting Miss Dynamite (Andrew). However, you can't help but be impressed with Jermaine's offering – his aunt is Olympic athlete Tessa Sanderson.

The band were an instant hit with the judges. However, things didn't go brilliantly and they were knocked out in the second week. The band are still keen to land a record deal and continue to play gigs up and down the country.

> 'I like you very much.'
> SHARON

4Sure

Donovan Bailey, Andrew Fisher, Kriss Jones, Jermaine Sanderson

From: West Midlands

Auditioned: Birmingham

Mentor: Louis / Groups

Audition songs: If You're Not the One; Yesterday

Judge's house song: I Swear

Songs sung at each stage of final:
1 What Becomes of the Broken Hearted
2 You're in My Heart

Final position: 11th

'You look absolutely fantastic.' LOUIS

Dionne Mitchell

Age: 26

From: London

Auditioned: London

Mentor: Sharon / Over 25s

Audition song: (You Make Me Feel Like) A Natural Woman

Judge's house song: What's Love Got to Do With it

Songs sung at each stage of final:
1 I'm Gonna Make You Love Me
2 Tonight's the Night
3 For Once in My Life

Final position: Joint 10th

Dionne Mitchell is the youngest of six children and developed a love of singing after joining a theatre company and performing in a play during her teens. Following the show she was asked to stay on at the company and went on to perform in clubs, as well as provide backing singing at concerts.

After nearly skipping *The X Factor* auditions due to nerves, it looked like Dionne was going to fall at the first hurdle during the auditions as Simon criticised her clothes, Louis didn't like her song choice and Sharon was a bit nonplussed. But in the end all three gave her the green light and she made it through to bootcamp. However, her joy soon turned to tears when she discovered that Sharon was to be her mentor as she felt that out of all the judges, she was the most critical of her.

On the first day of bootcamp Sharon exclaimed that she 'had a great personality', but Day Two didn't prove as positive with Sharon admitting that she wasn't sure if the public would warm to her. However, Dionne made it through the judges' houses round, and despite stalling mid-way through a performance, by the end of Day Two her cracking voice convinced Sharon that she was a goer.

After shedding a few more tears whilst she waited for the all-important 'yea' or 'nay' from Sharon, Dionne eventually let out a scream when she heard that she'd sung her way into the finals. Sadly she was eliminated in Week 3, but she is still busy performing at various gigs.

Kerry McGregor was left paraplegic and dependent on a wheelchair and crutches to get around after breaking her back falling out of a tree when she was 13. She was also a full-time mum when she auditioned for *The X Factor*.

It wasn't the first time she had sung competitively as she entered a *Song for Europe* in the hope of representing Britain in the Eurovision Song Contest in 1997. However, her track 'Yodel in the Canyon of Love' was beaten by Katrina and the Waves, whose song 'Love Shine a Light' went on to win the competition.

Kerry also sang on a dance track called 'Freedom' by QFX, which reached Number 23 in the UK, and appeared in three episodes of the Channel 4 comedy show *The Book Group* in 2003.

Kerry got a resounding 'yes' from all three judges during her audition, and after wowing Sharon both at bootcamp and during the judges' houses round, Sharon put her through to the live shows simply saying that her eyes sparkled and when she sang she loved her lust for life.

Kerry said that winning *The X Factor* would mean so much to her because, 'It would be a great sense of achievement because my life has been a bit of a toil and I've fought against so many difficulties... It would prove to me that everything I've ever done has been worth it and that I've always been fighting in the right direction.'

Although she didn't make it all the way, *The X Factor* got her beautiful voice recognised and she has been kept busy ever since.

Age: 31

From: West Lothian

Auditioned: Glasgow

Mentor: Sharon / Over 25s

Audition song: Show Me Heaven

Judge's house song: You've Got a Friend

Songs sung at each stage of final:
1 You Are the Sunshine of My Life
2 I Don't Want to Talk about It
3 They Can't Take That Away from Me

Final position: Joint 10th

'You deserve to be on that stage.' LOUIS

Kerry McGregor

As a former model for Topman, Ashley had already had a taste of fame and had a deal with the esteemed modelling agency Storm. One of five children, he was a keen gymnast and won medals for his skills. The judges loved him from the word go and Louis told him, 'You've got a great voice. We'll remember you.'

But when it came to the bootcamp stage, Simon was left feeling a little disappointed after his rendition of 'Be My Baby' by The Ronettes. 'I feel like I've backed a horse that won't go the distance. I thought if anyone could do it, he could. His phrasing was so bad,' admitted a worried Simon.

The pair also had words over Simon's choice of song for Ashley during the judges' houses round – George Michael's 'I Can't Make You Love Me' – meaning that Simon almost gave up on him. 'He's cocky, unreliable and all over the place,' he ranted. 'I worry about his reliability. Will he perform in the live shows?'

However, Sinitta admitted that she loved him and thought they should take a chance, and Ashley admitted that he did have a genuine desire to win. 'Winning would mean a lot to me,' he said. 'In fact, it would mean everything because it's the start of the beginning and it would mean the world.'

But Robert proved to be the better contender when they went up against each other in Week 4, and we had to wave goodbye to him and his lovely hair.

Ashley McKenzie

Age: 20

From: Croydon

Auditioned: Bristol

Mentor: Simon / 16–24s

Audition songs: Ribbon in the Sky; Holding Back the Years

Songs sung at judge's house: I Can't Make You Love Me; All in Love Is Fair

Songs sung at each stage of final:
1 Easy
2 I'd Rather Go Blind
3 Moondance
4 The Winner Takes It All

Final position: 8th

> ‘You have a great pureness about what you do.’ SHARON

Nikitta Angus

Nikitta Angus started singing at the tender age of seven, and was lucky enough to have someone to hold her hand throughout the tough audition process – her Aunt Katie also auditioned but failed to make it into Sharon's final 12.

Nikitta certainly needed the support. As if it's not scary enough having to face Simon, Louis and Sharon, the last time Nikitta planned to audition for *The X Factor* in 2005 she was knocked down by a car ten minutes before her audition.

Nikitta had tragically lost her mum to cancer the year before she auditioned and Simon bought tears to many people's eyes when he told her, 'The song was beautiful, your voice was great and your mum would be very proud of you.'

Simon remained a fan throughout the culling process, and when it came to making a decision during the judges' houses round he didn't have to think twice about putting her through saying, 'I loved her. She is so real and she lights up the room. I really want to go on the journey with her.'

And clearly she was just as eager to see the competition through saying, 'Winning *The X Factor* would be like a dream come true. Before my mum died she made me promise never to give up on my singing so I feel like I'm fulfilling her dying wish.'

Age: 17

From: Glasgow

Auditioned: Glasgow

Mentor: Simon / 16–24s

Audition songs: Drift Away; Dimming of the Day

Songs sung at judge's house: It's Too Late; Angels

Songs sung at each stage of final:
1 Heaven Must Have Sent You
2 Bring It on Home to Me
3 Sway
4 Dancing Queen
5 Last Dance

Final position: 7th

'Robert, you are what *The X Factor* is all about.' LOUIS

Robert Allen

Robert had a background in music before trying out for *The X Factor*, having been in two bands – The Continentals and Citizen K. He is also a professionally trained dancer, is trained in method acting and can play clarinet to grade 4.

He got a mixed reception during his first outing in front of the judges with Simon claiming it was a 'Jack of all trades audition. Quite good at anything. Not good at much.'

He made it through to bootcamp, but it looked worryingly like he'd messed things up during Day Two when he sang Prince's 'Purple Rain', and had to stop and start three times due to nerves.

Needless to say this left Sharon feeling frustrated and confused about what to do, but she gave him a second chance after his performance of Gnarls Barkley's 'Crazy' during the judges' houses round and convinced her he was worth a chance.

He got massive support from his girlfriend Samia during the show, but he admitted that it was hard moving away from her to appear on the show and that he missed her terribly. Robert has performed at a number of shows since appearing on *The X Factor* and plans to release an album.

Eton Road

Anthony Hannah, 17, Daniel Morris, 17, David Heath, 19, and James Edwards, 20, met while attending the Chiltern Casting dance school on Eton Road – which may give you a clue as to where they got their name...

The lads had spent a number of years performing in shows and cabarets and trying out in competitions before forming the band, which came to fruition just four days before their *X Factor* audition. Anthony previously appeared on *Stars in Their Eyes Kids* as Robbie Williams, and had also been on stage with Gareth Gates during one of his *Top of the Pops* appearances after winning the chance.

Louis initially had his reservations about the band and said on the first day of bootcamp, 'They're fresh, something new, I'm not massively disappointed. I just don't know what to do with them.'

In the end the lads got a 'no' from Louis, and were amazed when they were given a second chance after fellow boy band Avenue were disqualified.

The guys' fan base grew steadily during their time on the show and they have been regularly booked for performances following their departure. In early 2007 they signed a record deal with Sony BMG. Anthony left the band in August 2007 and the boys have just recruited a new member.

James Edwards, Anthony Hannah, David Heath and Daniel Morris

From: Liverpool

Auditioned: Manchester

Mentor: Louis / Groups

Audition songs: Changes in My Life; Lonely

Judge's house song: God Only Knows

Songs sung at each stage of final:
1 My Girl
2 This Old Heart of Mine
3 Mack the Knife
4 Does Your Mother Know?
5 From Me to You
6 I Don't Feel Like Dancin'
7 Can You Feel the Love Tonight; Everybody Needs Somebody To Love

Final position: 5th

'You're odd, unusual and that's what makes you stand out.' SIMON

'I feel guilty having a go at you. You're two lovely guys.' SHARON

The MacDonald Brothers

The MacDonald Brothers, 19-year-old Brian and 20-year-old Craig, began performing together from a young age. But rather than singing, the duo would play the accordion and the fiddle to keep family and friends amused. Even to this day they have a passion for musical instruments, and both the lads can play the piano and guitar.

They were largely influenced by their music-loving father, himself an accomplished guitarist, who taught them how to sing, perform and entertain. However, it was when they entered a school talent contest with their Queen tribute band Cobra that they realised singing was their future.

Both the lads cite Freddie Mercury as one of their biggest influences and say that he inspired them to start performing, while they also rate the likes of Eric Clapton, Phil Collins, Elton John, Scissor Sisters and The Red Hot Chilli Peppers.

They began performing professionally as a duo three years ago, and before *The X Factor* they did the rounds of weddings, clubs and bars and also occasionally did backing singing for other bands. One of their biggest gigs pre-*X Factor* was performing at the Ceilidh Dance in front of none other than actor Hugh Grant.

'What we're not seeing is potential star quality.' SIMON

Brian MacDonald and Craig MacDonald

From: Ayr, Scotland

Auditioned: Glasgow

Mentor: Louis / Groups

Audition songs: Don't Worry Baby; As Long As You Love Me

Judge's house song: All I Have to Do Is Dream

Songs sung at each stage of final:
1 Three Times a Lady
2 Sailing
3 Can't Take My Eyes off You
4 Fernando
5 She's the One
6 Love Is All Around
7 When You Say Nothing at All
8 Can't Smile without You; Shang-a-Lang

Final position: 4th

The brothers had their fair share of mundane jobs while they dreamed of reaching the top of the charts, and while Craig worked in a bar and in an ice-cream shop, Brian became an administrator meaning that he had to do 'a nine-to-five, which entailed me staring at a computer screen'.

The pair were ecstatic when they made it through to the finals of *The X Factor* with Brian saying, 'It would mean everything we've worked for has paid off. This is a stepping-stone to our dreams. It's what we've always wanted to do.'

But while their mentor Louis championed the band throughout the series, Simon was much less keen and would routinely question why they were even on the show. Many thought that this actually prompted more people to vote for the guys, and they managed to make it all the way to Week 8 before being eliminated.

Now going under the name Macdonald Bros, the duo released their first single, a cover of the Bay City Rollers' 'Shang-a-Lang' in April 2007, while their self-titled debut album went to Number 18 in the UK charts. They also supported Westlife on tour in 2007 and are consistently busy playing gigs around the UK.

'You've given an amazing performance tonight.' LOUIS

'That was outstanding.' SIMON

Ben Mills

Age: 26

From: Kent

Auditioned: London

Mentor: Sharon / Over 25s

Audition song: Bring It Home

Judge's house song: With a Little Help from My Friends

Songs sung at each stage of final:
1 Tracks of My Tears
2 Maggie May
3 Smile
4 S.O.S.
5 Don't Wanna Miss a Thing
6 With a Little Help from My Friends
7 Your Song; Live and Let Die
8 I Made It through the Rain; Somebody to Love
9 (Everything I Do) I Do It for You; I Still Haven't Found What I'm Looking For

Final position: 3rd

Thanks to his gravely voice and rocky style, Ben Mills was compared to the likes of Joe Cocker and Rod Stewart during his time on *The X Factor* – something which Ben, as a huge fan of both, was particularly pleased about. The judges said his unique sound made him stand out from the crowd, and he was soon having praise heaped upon him from music critics across the land.

Before trying out for *The X Factor*, Ben was the co-director of a marquee company in Whitstable. Other previous jobs included driving a tractor on a strawberry farm and working on a building site. But whatever he was doing he had always dreamed of a career in his number one love – music.

Having sung since he was a child, he started taking the prospect of forging a career in the record industry more seriously during his teens. He later gained a diploma in music from the Academy of Contemporary Music in Guildford and went on to become a keyboard player in The L.A. Doors, a tribute band to The Doors, playing to over 8,000 people during a tour of Europe. The talented guitarist also toured clubs and bars with his own band, Benzego.

After making it through to the finals, Ben said that winning *The X Factor* would be, 'Everything I've ever wanted and more. It's the direction my life needs to take at the moment and it would mean so much to me.'

Ben may not have made it all the way, but his appearances on the show caught the eye of Sony BMG who offered him a five-album record deal after the show.

His debut offering, 'Picture of You', was an eclectic mix of covers of classic songs from the likes of Rod Stewart, Aerosmith and Queen, and brand-new material. He famously released the album on the same day as his former stage mate Ray Quinn on 12 March 2007, which resulted in Ray nudging ahead of him to steal the top spot in the charts while Ben scored a very respectable Number 3. The album is already certified platinum and Ben is making plans for the follow-up.

As well as his album release, Ben has made numerous TV appearances, has been busy gigging around the UK at clubs and festivals and in 2007 appeared as a guest singer on an episode of *Chucklevision*. Strange, but true.

Raymond Quinn

Age: 18

From: Liverpool

Auditioned: Birmingham

Mentor: Simon / 16–24s

Audition song: Ain't That a Kick in the Head

Songs sung at judge's house: She's the One; Smile

Songs sung at each stage of final:
1 Ben
2 What a Wonderful World
3 Ain't That a Kick in the Head
4 Waterloo
5 Crazy Little Thing Called Love
6 Livin' La Vida Loca
7 The Way You Look Tonight; Jailhouse Rock
8 Mandy; My Way
9 Smile; You'll Never Walk Alone
Final: My Way; Fly Me to the Moon; A Moment Like This

Final position: 2nd

When a cute young lad walked into the audition room in Birmingham, many viewers sensed that there was something familiar about him – they just couldn't put their finger on where they'd seen it before. And a collective 'ah-haa' could be heard around the country when it was revealed that *The X Factor* auditions weren't the first time Ray had graced our TV screens, having starred as Anthony Murray for several years in the popular Channel 4 soap *Brookside*.

He was best known for the dramatic storyline which involved him killing a teenage girl because he was being bullied, and the scenes brought him much recognition from the soap world. He walked away with three awards in 2002 – Best Dramatic Performance and Best Storyline at the British Soap Awards and Best Young Actor at the Inside Soap Awards.

In addition to *Brookside*, Ray also appeared in *The Afternoon Play*, *Doctors* and a children's show called *Cactus Jack* before trying out for *The X Factor*.

Directly before the show he was a student at the Merseyside Dance and Drama College. He still had a year to go as a student but dropped out following his success on *The X Factor*.

As he was the youngest in the competition, everyone fell in love with Ray from the word go with Simon describing him as 'charming' and 'likeable' and all judges giving him the thumbs up for the bootcamp round during his audition. However, he nearly missed out on a place in the live shows when Simon initially excluded him from his final seven during the bootcamp stages, and it was only after he begged producers to let him put eight instead of seven acts through to the judges' houses round that he secured his place.

Ray said that winning *The X Factor* would, 'Change my life completely. It'd be a dream come true to become a recording artist. The first things I would buy would be a car and a house!'

'You keep coming back stronger than ever.'
SHARON

Although he eventually lost out to Leona in the finals, Ray signed a deal with Sony BMG on 16 January 2007 and was thrilled when he got to go to the world-famous Capitol Records Tower in LA to record a swing album. It went to Number 1 on its release on 12 March 2007, and was certified gold in its first week.

Ray also scored a huge record contract to advertise hair creams and gels due to his finely coiffured locks. His first solo tour took place in October 2007, and he is already working on his second album.

'You own the stage, you're a great showman.' LOUIS

The judges were stunned when a quiet, shy Leona Lewis walked into the audition room and began to sing 'Over the Rainbow'. Her note-perfect voice made them all sit up and listen and she was put through to the next round with unanimous 'yes'es.

She was a firm favourite throughout the audition process and live shows, and few people were surprised when she was announced as the overall winner after a whopping eight million votes were cast. In fact, Simon even commented to her, 'You are absolutely the best contestant I have ever had across any of these shows.' High praise indeed.

Leona has had a lifelong passion for singing. She wrote her first song when she was 12, and aged 13 she won the Lady D Under-18 talent show at London's Hackney Empire. She later attended the famous BRIT School, and directly before entering *The X Factor*, she worked as a receptionist, spending all her spare time working on music and putting together demos. She admits that she had to sacrifice her social life to spend time in the studio. But needless to say, she now feels that her hard work has well and truly paid off!

Leona released her debut single 'A Moment Like This' on 20 December 2006. It sold an amazing 571,000 copies in its first week of release – more than the rest

'It is so endearing to find somebody who has such a huge voice as you.' SHARON

of the top forty's sales combined – and instantly became the most downloaded song of 2006, beating Gnarls Barkley's massive hit 'Crazy' into second place. It also went on to scoop an esteemed Ivor Novello award for Best Selling UK Single.

Two thousand and seven proved to be every bit as exciting for Leona as she signed a £5-million contract in America with legendary music mogul Clive Davis, which will see her release five albums. She spent much of the beginning of the year in LA working on her debut album with the cream of the world's producing talents, such as Dallas Austin, Jimmy Jam and Terry Lewis.

In March 2007 Leona sang for royalty at The Prince's Trust & RBS Celebrate Success Awards, where she performed 'Over the Rainbow' in front of none other than Prince Charles himself. She released her much-anticipated debut album in the autumn of 2007 to huge critical acclaim.

INTERVIEW WITH LEONA
How was your *X Factor* experience?
I guess I didn't realise how life-changing it was going to be for me. I've come out learning that you have to seize every opportunity. Every missed opportunity could be the thing that changes your life. It was an incredible experience and one I'll never forget.

What made you decide to enter?
I watched the previous shows and thought it was such great entertainment and such a great show for people to showcase themselves on. At the time I was trying to do the usual route of doing demos, and getting studio time and sending stuff to record companies, but my boyfriend said that I should apply. He said that if I would he would, so we went and did it together.

Leona Lewis

Age: 21

From: London

Auditioned: London

Mentor: Simon / 16–24s

Audition song: Over the Rainbow

Songs sung at judge's house: You Light Up My Life; Without You

Songs sung at each stage of final:
1 I'll Be There
2 The First Cut Is the Deepest
3 Summertime
4 Chiquitita
5 Sorry Seems to Be the Hardest Word
6 Bridge over Troubled Water
7 Lady Marmalade; I Will Always Love You
8 Could It Be Magic; Without You
9 I Have Nothing; Somewhere over the Rainbow
Final: I Will Always Love You; All by Myself;
    A Moment Like This

Final position: 1st

How did you find the auditions?

It was really nerve-wracking but my boyfriend and my dad came with me to support me and that really helped me.

Were you surprised when you got through?

Yes, you never know what people are looking for. I think my choice of song and the fact that I was coming from a place that was honest really helped me. All I could do was be myself. I see myself as a genuine person and I wasn't going with an ulterior motive. I just wanted to sing and I think the judges saw that and put me through.

How did you feel when your name was read out as the winner of the show?

That moment was just incredible. Ray came over and picked me up, and I always say that ever since then my feet haven't touched the ground. It's been amazing and I feel so grateful and so blessed to have done this.

How has winning changed your life?

It's changed it in so many ways. Being recognised for being a singer and being able to work with such talented musicians and producers is amazing. I've been given the greatest opportunity and I know it sounds cheesy, but my dreams have definitely come true. It's a lot of travelling and different things, but it's so exciting and it's what I want to do. I wake up every morning and thank God; I'm just so thankful for where I'm at. I don't take anything for granted.

Who have you stayed friends with from the show?

Mainly Rob, Nikitta, Ashley, Eton Road and Ray. They're the people I regularly text and talk to. We did the tour together which was such a laugh. I'm so pleased with how Ray's done. He's an outstanding performer and personality and he deserves all the success he gets.

How do you see the future?

I'm really excited about the album being released. That's what I'm looking forward to most. It's going to be an amazing experience like winning the show and having a Number One single all over again. I can't wait.

'You are absolutely the best contestant I've ever had.' SIMON

INTERVIEW WITH LOUIS

How has this series been so far?
I think it's going to be the biggest series we've had, and I think it's going to be the best. We have four judges now and we all know we have to raise our game. Audition-wise there have been lots of loonies, and lots of talent.

Can you tell us about some of them?
Let's just say that the crazies are really crazy. Some days we would sit there and wonder where they came from. Some of them have got absolutely no talent – none! They can't even hold a tune. We had a lot of sob stories of people singing for people who have died. All human life is there this year but there really is a handful of talent in each category. Every time someone great came in it would absolutely make our day because we had so many bad people. Some people came in so unprepared and unrehearsed and sing the same old songs.

Which songs are you sick of?
We had a lot of Maroon 5, James Morrison and Snow Patrol this year, and also Michael Bublé. We had a lot of girls trying to sing like Whitney or Mariah, and boys trying to sing like Al Green. Why would you do that? It never, ever works. They watch this show so they should think about it! As Simon says, it's hard enough for good people to sell records, so what chance have they got if they're bad?

Did you have lots of sobbers?
Everyone was crying. Even I was nearly crying when I had to tell a young kid he didn't get through. But we can't put people through because they cry, we have to put the good people through. Everyone is so emotional because they just want it so badly.

How is it having Dannii on board?
I thought it was strange at the start but I think it's a good thing because we have to work harder. Our reputations are on the line. Sharon would usually agree with me on things in the past, but we're all having to up our games. Dannii is much better than I thought she would be. I think Simon's smugness is rubbing off on her a bit though, and she's very confident! She's been in the business for twenty-seven years and she likes music and she knows what she's doing. I'm surprised by how good she is. She's a thousand times better than I expected and she's improving all the time. She's absolutely great.

Have there been many rows between the judges?
Not too many so far, but the competition is getting more serious. We have our categories and everyone wants to win so there are plenty of egos. There are four of us and we do take it seriously. I'm not pleased with my category as it's not the one I wanted, but I do have two good people in it. They deliberately gave me the category I didn't want – they set me up! I still think I can win though and I'm going to fight to the bitter end.

How are you getting along with Dermot?
I like Dermot, I think he's the best male presenter out there. He's fitting in so well and he's a genuinely nice guy. He was shocked by how seriously we take it all though!

You must be pleased that you're back on the show after your earlier exit?
Oh yes, I was devastated when I was axed and I didn't even hesitate when I was asked back. I said 'yes' immediately. They should never have got rid of me in the first place as we all have such a great chemistry. We get on so well.

What are you proudest of when you look back at all the series so far?
Shayne Ward. I think he's a proper star. Everything about him oozes star quality – his voice, his work ethic, everything. I'm also proud of G4 because they sold one point four million records. And the McDonald Brothers have a Number One album in Ireland and they're still working off the back of this show. It's an amazing platform for the right person. And I do think Leona is going to be a big, big star. The show is all about people like Shayne and Leona.

What's your hope for this series?
I would like to get the winner, but then the hard work starts. I need someone who is going to have a career and sell records, not just one album. I want to be able to really launch someone. Honestly, there are twelve great acts, although I did put through a couple of people just to annoy Simon. Sharon and I always do it just because we hope he'll get them in their category because we know it will drive him up the wall.

What are you most looking forward to?
I want this show to be bigger and better than last year. I'm going to be very competitive and I don't want to lose acts. I want to be better than all the other judges. I'm in it to win and that's it. I don't like losing – especially to any of the other judges.

115

SERIES FOUR

THE EARLY STAGES

AS WITH PREVIOUS YEARS, the Series Four auditions attracted the great, the good and the downright crazy – with a few surprises to boot! And as we all know, nothing makes the judges happier than a whole bunch of bizarre contestants. Ahem.

The auditions covered London, Sheffield, Glasgow, Manchester, Birmingham, Belfast and Cardiff and things got off to a, er, cracking start at North London's Emirates Stadium. The very first person to audition is 55-year-old Susan Perkins who boasts beforehand that, 'When I walk back through these doors I hope I'm going to be a superstar.' After telling the judges 'I've wanted to be a singer ever since I was a little girl and I would just love to be able to achieve my ambition today,' she launches into her very own interpretation of 'You'll Never Walk Alone'. And it isn't long before the panel are wishing that she was singing in a room on her own. Her 'interesting' take on the classic has Simon et al in stitches. And while she happily claims that she enjoyed her performance, newcomer Brian Friedman is forced to admit, 'It wasn't really my cup of tea.'

Among the other highlights are 70-year-old Emily, who auditions with a scarf over her face to hide her dodgy teeth (although she is particularly complimentary about Simon's gnashers, telling him, 'Simon you're a warm, charismatic, handsome

person with good dentistry. But that doesn't give you the right to tell me that *I* need to get dentistry'). After coming in to criticism from Simon and a flurry of firm 'no's she leaves the room claiming that 'Simon got out of bed the wrong side this morning.'

Other memorable auditionees are Johnny Rocco, who comes across as a lovable granddad figure – until he gets 'no's from the judges, at which point he starts handing out scary threats. And Joy, with her imaginary instruments, lives up to her name and puts a smile on all the judges' faces (at least we *think* Simon was smiling).

In London, Simon and Dannii have the first of many clashes over girl band W4. While Simon is far from a fan, saying they aren't original, Dannii stands up for them, arguing 'I absolutely disagree with you. The unity and your energy is amazing. It's like I want to be in your gang, I want to go wherever you go next because you look like you're going to have fun!'

Brother-and-sister act Same Difference, a.k.a. Sarah and Sean Smith, leave all the judges wide-eyed, thanks to their boundless enthusiasm. But sadly the panel aren't quite as keen about their talent or their take on The Rembrandts' 'I'll Be There for You'. A deadpan Simon advises them to calm down, telling them that they need to watch some depressing documentaries and comments, 'OK, can we lose the crazy faces, the screaming, the shouting? Because this is just so insane at the moment. You are so funny you two! God, I pity your parents. I bet you both wake up in great moods.' But when Brian agrees and suggests that they could be a touch less enthusiastic, Dannii jumps to their defence saying, 'I don't think these guys *can* tone it down and I don't think you should. You guys do that so well and you're so adorable and lovable and you should keep doing that. But it's not an *X Factor* winner.'

Without a doubt, some of the most terrifying contestants from 2007 are professional funeral singers and identical twins Michelle and Julie Croghan, who pop along to bring a little bit of joy and happiness to the Belfast auditions. It was never going to go brilliantly after Dannii mistakes them for men and Simon accuses them of wearing wigs, but they still do their best and kick off by announcing that, 'The undertakers have been pushing us to come and audition. Everyone whose funerals we have sung at have said that we've made their day!' But unfortunately their performance of Sarah McLachlan's 'Angel' doesn't make the judges' days and Simon quips, 'I've got to be honest girls, I'd want to throw myself in the coffin after that.' Still, Sharon does announce that she'd like to make an advance booking for her funeral, which is always a cheery way to end a terrible audition!

Cardiff-native Rachel Lester manages to terrify even tough Sharon with her terrible attitude and hostile manner. Following her disastrous audition she gives the judges a mouthful using all

manner of profanities, after which Sharon comments 'What an ugly, ugly person. In four years we've never had anyone that out-there and abusive come in to the room, she was so full of hatred and she even scared me.'

Kerry Northall, while not quite so scary, but definitely slightly on the insistent side, thinks 'I've not just got the "X Factor", I've got the "Wow Factor". The "X Factor" is me. I may not have the looks but I have got the "X Factor". I'm like Celine Dion, Whitney and Mariah, I'd give my vocals ten out of ten,' she explains to the judges, shortly before a truly terrible performance of Whitney Houston's 'I Will Always Love You'. After getting a resounding thumbs down, she storms out of the room and in a matter of minutes, her dad thunders in asking Simon to give her a second chance. But his cries fall on deaf ears. Still, Kelly gets to have the final say outside the room when she rants to the cameras, 'He's the nastiest person I've ever met and I'll prove him wrong, you just wait and see!'

Ambitious Zoe is certain she is going to make the grade, but her rendition of Christina Aguilera's 'Beautiful' prompts Simon to say, 'It was terrible.' And as much as she tries to argue her case, she is still shown the door and then starts to, erm, bang her head against the nearest wall.

However, thankfully there is a smattering of genuine talent in the shape of Nikki Evans, 14-year-old Emily – who is the show's youngest-ever contestant – 15-year-old Paris Jones, who is back for her second go at the competition, 23-year-old Richard Wilkinson and girl band Fallen Angelz.

Twenty-year-old Sam Donaghey finds a fan in Dannii when he sings 'Handbags and Gladrags', after which she enthuses, 'I love your voice and its tone, I think you could sparkle. I love you, I think you're fantastic.'

There isn't a dry eye in the house when single mum Natasha and her seven-year-old daughter Jasmine go along to the Birmingham auditions. Having escaped from a violent relationship, Natasha is auditioning in a bid to give her daughter a better life. 'We've been through a lot over the past couple of years. Right now feels like a turning point for me and I want her to see her mum actually achieve and get further in life,' she tells the transfixed room. Her rendition of Toni Braxton's 'Un-Break My Heart' gets a full set of 'yes'es – including one from Jasmine who is invited to join the judging panel – giving her the break she's been hoping for, and a chance to shine in the bootcamp stage.

Meanwhile, brilliant 15-year-old Dominic tells the judges, 'In school we were asked to write down where we wanted to be in five years time. And at the top of my list was to have a number one album and a number one single; just to fulfil my dreams. Singing means everything to me and I've had so much support from all the family and I really want to do this for my mum and my nan.' And who knows? His dreams may well come true after Simon says of his belting performance of 'Mack the Knife', 'Wow, you are one talented young man. For someone like you to come in, you look so hip, you've got great taste in music and you are your own person, it's really, really refreshing.'

But of course, the biggest star of the audition stages is Mr Louis Walsh. The lovable judge makes his big return to the show during episode one, having been sacked just weeks earlier. Realising that the show simply wasn't the same without him, Simon begged Louis to come back to the winning line-up, replacing Brian Friedman who happily took on a role as the show's creative director. And it didn't take long for Simon and Louis to get back to their old bickering selves. Hurrah!

123

BOOTCAMP

THE X FACTOR'S BOOTCAMP STAGE got a bit of a shake-up for Series Four, which came as a shock to the contestants. In the past, the judges have always held separate bootcamps as each judge had already been allocated their category. However, this time around *all* the judges saw *all* of the auditionees lucky enough to get through to this stage. And all had a say on who should go through – kind of like a super-bootcamp! The other big twist was that there were four categories instead of the usual three – Boys Aged 14–24, Girls Aged 14–24, Groups and Over 25s.

Firstly, all four judges and 250 bootcamp contestants decamped to a beautiful stately home called Heythrop Park House in Oxfordshire for an intense four-day singing session. Small stages were set up in different rooms of the house so the contestants could sing for the judges in an intimate space.

Love affairs blossomed, contestants went skinny dipping in the swimming pool and a good time was had by... well, some. Simon complained after his beauty sleep was interrupted by people practising in the grounds, while there were tears from people who found the whole shebang a touch too stressful.

After four days of tough deliberations, the 250 were then whittled down to 50 finalists who were ferried by coach to a mystery location in London for the second section of bootcamp. Their destination

was the Apollo Theatre on Shaftesbury Avenue, where most of them got their first chance to appear on a stage in the glare of the spotlight as they showcased their talents.

The judges then chose their favourite six in each category, who would then go on to the all-important judges' houses stage. And as none of the judges had any idea which grouping they were getting, their decisions were totally impartial.

It was only once the final 24 had been chosen that the judges discovered which category they had been given. The

finalists for each were put into separate rooms and the judges were handed an envelope instructing them to go to a certain room. And so, as soon as they got there, they found out who they were going to be mentoring.

Dannii was thrilled about getting the Boys Aged 14–24, Simon was very happy to be handed the Groups, Sharon was excited about getting the Girls Aged 14–24, while Louis was gutted to get the Over 25s. But he soon came round to the idea after discovering that his category harboured a lot more talent than he'd bargained for...

THE JUDGES' HOUSES

WITH THE FINAL 24 contestants chosen, it was time to head to the judges' houses where everyone was to discover which three acts from each category would make it to the live shows.

As ever, there were some glamorous locations involved, with Sharon's acts jetting off to fabulous LA and Simon's lucky lot going to sunny Marbella. Dannii's got to hang in beautiful Ibiza, while Louis headed to his home town of Dublin. And while they may not have had the sun, they did get the Guinness...

As with every year, each judge also took along an expert to help them make their all-important decisions. Sharon had Nicole from the Pussycat Dolls as her beautiful assistant; Sinitta, one of Simon's closest friends, made a welcome return to help him out; Louis enlisted the expertise of Westlife's Kian; and newcomer Dannii also chose well, roping in top writer and producer Terry Rowland to work alongside her.

There were a couple of surprises in Simon's Groups because – yes – there was yet another twist! For the first time ever, groups were made up from some of the solo artists who made it through to bootcamp. Although it hadn't been planned, during the bootcamp stage the judges realised that there were some incredibly talented people who may not cut it as solo singers, but who would be perfect as part of a group. So Louis came up with the brilliant idea of giving artists – who had been turned down as soloists – the chance to form bands.

They were given 24 hours to practise together, and then they were back before the judges in the hope of getting through to the final 12. And Louis' idea certainly proved to be a brilliant one when several of the bands made the grade!

The first day of the judges' houses round were when all the acts – including the all-new band line-ups! – got to try and impress the judges. After having a chance to sleep on it, the judges then had to deliver the good – or bad – news to the aspiring singers.

In a matter of minutes each and every person discovered their fate from their mentor and found out whether they had cut it, or whether they had simply been cut. And with a million-pound record deal on offer, needless to say it wasn't long before the tears started flowing...

SERIES FOUR

BOYS AGED 14–24

Andy Williams

Age: 22

From: Newport, South Wales

Auditioned: Cardiff

Mentor: Dannii

Audition song: Fly Me to the Moon

Judge's house songs: Sorry Seems to Be the Hardest Word; You're Beautiful

Songs sung at each stage of final:

Final position:

This wasn't the first time that 22-year-old Andy tried out for *The X Factor*. The budding singer auditioned for the very first series three years ago when he was 19, but sadly he didn't make it past the first stage. But undeterred, he has spent the past three years practising his singing and honing his dance moves in various local clubs. So he was back this year to try his luck again.

He celebrated making it through to the bootcamp stage by getting a tattoo on his bottom which reads 'music', and is identical to one that his dad and brother both have!

He lives at home with his mum, dad and 25-year-old brother, Lee, and prior to trying out for *The X Factor*, the brothers have been running their own asbestos removal company for four years.

Leon Jackson

Age: 18

From: West Lothian, Scotland

Auditioned: Glasgow

Mentor: Dannii

Audition songs: Stay with You; Home

Judge's house songs: I Still Haven't Found What I'm Looking For; Chasing Cars

Songs sung at each stage of final:

Final position:

Leon, most recently a sales assistant in Gap, is an only child who was brought up in West Lothian by his mum, a single parent. His mum battled financial difficulties while bringing Leon up and he admitted from the word go that he was hoping to win *The X Factor* so that he could provide them both with a better life. It was his mum who set him on the road to stardom when she bought him an iPod and he started recording songs on it. After playing his offerings to friends, they dragged him to local karaoke nights where he began impressing people on a wider scale, and he was soon hooked!

Leon is a black belt in karate, loves modern jazz and highly rates Michael Bublé and Jamie Cullum. Before auditioning for *The X Factor*, Leon was planning to do an Architectural Technology course at university, but needless to say that got put on hold after he made it through to the finals...

Age: 24

From: Powys, Wales

Auditioned: Birmingham

Mentor: Dannii

Audition songs: Love to Me; Danny Boy

Judge's house songs: Somebody to Love; All by Myself

Songs sung at each stage of final:

Final position:

Rhydian Roberts

Welsh native Rhydian currently lives with friends in Birmingham where he is a student in vocal studies at university, and a personal trainer. The 24-year-old is a classical baritone singer and has had vocal training for the past seven years. He sings popular opera songs in a similar style to Il Divo and Russell Watson, and the confident chap is convinced that if he were to record and release an album 'the whole of Wales would buy it'. He also says that he plans to use *The X Factor* to bring his style of music to the masses!

And singing isn't his only skill – in his younger years Rhydian was the strongest bench-presser in Wales, but he gave up weightlifting in his early teens when he realised that his premier passion was music.

131

SERIES FOUR

GIRLS

AGED

14–24

Alisha was a big fan of last year's *X Factor* winner Leona Lewis, who inspired Alisha to follow her dream of becoming a singer. That, and the fact that she lives around the corner from *The X Factor*'s Wembley studio and every time she saw the crowds of fans queuing, she thought to herself, 'I'll have some of that!'

Alisha's musical background has been based largely around her church's gospel choir, and she has spent the last year having singing lessons in a bid to be ready for the competition.

She is incredibly close to her mum, Sharon, and describes them as 'Ab Fab' after the flamboyant TV characters, as they are both equally loud and entertaining.

As well as singing, Alisha is passionate about fashion and loves catching up on all the latest trends and gossip in glossy fashion magazines. She also once worked as a style advisor in Top Shop, so she knows what she likes – and what she doesn't!

Alisha Bennett

Age: 23

From: Wembley, London

Auditioned: London

Mentor: Sharon

Audition songs: Sweetest Hangover; Killing Me Softly

Judge's house songs: Chains; I Try

Songs sung at each stage of final:

Final position:

Kimberley Southwick

Age: 19

From: Tamworth, West Midlands

Auditioned: Birmingham

Mentor: Sharon

Audition songs: Redneck Woman;
Show Me Heaven

Judge's house songs: Girls Just Want to
Have Fun; I'll Stand by You

Songs sung at each stage of final:

Final position:

Kimberley had plenty of chances to practise singing before auditioning for *The X Factor* – she regularly performed in her parents' pub, where she would entertain customers with her belting renditions of country music songs! She also works in the pub, The Fox in Tamworth, having quit her job in a call centre because she found it boring (we assume she wasn't allowed to sing on the job then).

She attended London's esteemed Italia Conti stage school for a year but left because she 'didn't enjoy it', and has also performed on Michael Barrymore's My Kind of People. But her worst (or best, depending on how you look at it) job ever was when she had to dress up as an elf one Christmas, and help out in Santa's grotto.

Emily Nakanda

Age: 15

From: North London

Auditioned: London

Mentor: Sharon

Audition song: Almaz

Judge's house songs: Beautiful;
I'm Like a Bird

Songs sung at each stage of final:

Final position:

Many people remembered Emily during the auditions as she was the first ever 14-year-old to sing for the judges after the age limit was lowered for this series. The judges were left open-mouthed after her incredible rendition of Randy Crawford's 'Almaz', which prompted Simon to declare that she was the reason why the age range was lowered.

Emily loves all kinds of music and has sung in her school and church choirs. She lives in North London with her mum, step-dad and older brother, Terry. Her caring family say that they feel 'very blessed to have her with us' after she fell ill with the serious condition peritonitis last year.

SERIES FOUR

OVER 25s

Beverley started singing at the tender age of just four and the finals weren't the first time she appeared on *The X Factor* stage. She is a member of the award-winning Kingdom Choir, who have performed as backing vocalists on both *The X Factor* and *Grease Is the Word*!

Beverley is a primary school teacher who lives in Luton with her proud husband, Jonathan, and their two children, 12-year-old Tianna and 10-year-old Luke. Beverley isn't the only member of her family who has been on television – one of her nephews, Leon Barnett, plays football for West Bromwich.

Beverley Trottman

Age: 37

From: Luton, Beds

Auditioned: Cardiff

Mentor: Louis

Audition song: Respect

Judge's house songs: (You Make Me Feel Like) A Natural Woman; When You Tell Me That You Love Me

Songs sung at each stage of final:

Final position:

Nikki Evans

Age: 34

From: Tamworth, West Midlands

Auditioned: Birmingham

Mentor: Louis

Audition songs: Fields of Gold; I Will Always Love You

Judge's house songs: One Moment in Time; We've Only Just Begun

Songs sung at each stage of final:

Final position:

Nikki applied for *The X Factor* after discovering the application form in her recently deceased, beloved father's belongings. He had been her biggest supporter, having gone along to every gig she'd ever done, so she decided to take part in the show in honour of his memory.

She has a solid musical history and has been in bands since she was 12; at the age of 16 she was even signed to Pete Waterman Limited. But sadly chart success didn't follow and her experience dented her confidence and caused her to question her singing ability. Her hope is that by appearing on *The X Factor* she will be able to recover some of her self-belief. Nikki is a catering manager at a school and lives in Tamworth with her husband, Darren, and their sons Morgan, 12, and Jonah, 10.

Daniel has been a dancer for most of his life and trained at the Royal Ballet School from the age of 11. When he was 17, he landed a job as a professional dancer for the esteemed Rambert Dance Company. He stayed with them for four years, until sadly he had to give up on his dream after sustaining a serious knee injury.

In 2001, Daniel landed a record contract with DreamWorks in America and worked with R. Kelly, but after the company was bought out, his single was shelved and he saw another dream crumble before his eyes.

He moved back to the UK and, before auditioning for *The X Factor*, was teaching dance and ballet and modelling. He lives with friends in London and has a three-year-old son, Theron, who he sees regularly.

Daniel De Bourg

Age: 31

From: London

Auditioned: London

Mentor: Louis

Audition songs: Three Times a Lady; When Doves Cry

Judge's house songs: One; Cannonball

Songs sung at each stage of final:

Final position:

SERIES FOUR
GROUPS

Brother-and-sister duo Sean, 21, and Sarah, 18, didn't get off to the best start during their first audition, with Simon declaring that they were two of the most annoying people he'd met. But they soon won him over and managed to make it all the way to the finals.

The pair live with their mum, dad and gran in Portsmouth and both have something of a showbiz background. Sean is an entertainer; he left home when he was 17 to work on cruise ships and also performed in a number of pantomimes. Sarah attended London's Italia Conti stage school, has also done some modelling and is currently a student.

Sean and Sarah regularly perform at their local old people's home and their dream is to win *The X Factor* so they can entertain the world!

Same Difference

Sarah Smith, Sean Smith

Auditioned: London

Mentor: Simon

Audition songs: I'll Be There for You; Baby When You're Gone

Judge's house songs: Nothing's Gonna Stop Us Now; You've Got a Friend

Songs sung at each stage of final:

Final position:

Futureproof

Adam Chandler, Aaron Delahunty, Matthew Protheroe, Sean Rumsey, Richard Wilkinson

Mentor: Simon

Judge's house songs: I Want it That Way; Nobody Knows

Songs sung at each stage of final:

Final position:

The lads originally auditioned for *The X Factor* as solo contestants, but they were given the opportunity to form a boy band during the bootcamp stage and jumped at the chance.

Adam, 21, was born and raised in Kent. He attended the BRIT School, has been singing for eleven years and now does it professionally, considering himself incredibly lucky to be making money doing what he loves.

Aaron, a 19-year-old Londoner, has made money busking around Covent Garden since the age of 10. He has been in numerous bands and can rap, dance, song-write and produce. He is hugely passionate about music and is a very determined fella.

Matthew, 17, lives in London. He attended the Sylvia Young Theatre School and has already had some experience in the music business, having sung backing vocals for Westlife and appeared in the West End show *Ragtime: The Musical*.

The X Factor isn't Sean's first foray into musical talent contests – in 2003 he got through to the finals of *Teen Idol*, and in 2006 he made it to the bootcamp stage of *The X Factor* as part of a duo called Ste and Sean. Now 20 years old, Sean grew up in a small town in Warwickshire and has been singing for eight years.

Richard, 23, was born and raised in Leeds. He has always loved singing but started taking it seriously in his early teens. He used to spend nights lying awake dreaming of being on stage, so making it all the way to the finals is literally his dream come true.

Hope

After each of them individually got a 'no' from the judges, the girls were thrilled at Bootcamp when they were given a second chance and allowed to form a girl band. Simon was a big fan from the beginning and liked their feistiness, but also advised them to lose their attitude.

Emily, 17, from Torquay, was inspired to audition for *The X Factor* after she sung for Sharon and Louis during an ad break for The *Sharon Osbourne Show*. She got a round of applause from both, so she decided to give it a go!

Phoebe is the youngest member of the band at 16, and has just finished her GCSEs. She lives in Surrey, sings, loves all forms of performing and at weekends has been attending the Guildford School of Acting.

Raquelle, 20, was born and raised in Manchester but now lives in London. She studied at the famous Italia Conti stage school for three years and is a budding singer and actress, previously appearing in a couple of plays.

Twenty-year-old Leah lives in London and is heavily into spirituality. She has always loved singing and is constantly searching for inspiring female vocalists to look up to. But alas she hasn't found any, and hopes she can fill that gap.

Before making it through to *The X Factor* finals, Charlie, 23, was all geared up for her new career in beauty therapy. She lives in Sunderland with her partner Lee and five-year-old son Jack, who she is hoping to make very proud!

Emily Biggs, Phoebe Brown, Raquelle Gracie, Leah Lauder, Charlie Mole

Mentor: Simon

Judge's house songs: Never Ever; Umbrella

Songs sung at each stage of final:

Final position:

How did the auditions go?

They were amazing. *Amazing.* However, a lot of people I call my Gary Larsons – they're on the Far Side! They're on their own little planet, having fun in their own universe. But they're all really good fun. As a fan of the show, I would always tune in to see the peculiar contestants rather than see the people who were really talented. You always get everything at auditions. You can get 14,000 people coming along in one day, so you really do get all sorts.

Who has been the strangest person you had coming along to the auditions?

We had a lady called Susan. She sang a whole song and brought me to tears! She was so funny that when I laughed my tears sprung out vertically, not downwards like when you're sad. I really tried not to laugh, but in the end all four judges were laughing. One of the crew

members said to me afterwards that it's the first time that he's seen all the judges lose it at the same time. I think she thought she was at Wembley or something though. She was in the zone. And a guy called Dwayne I loved too. He's an inventor and he's making a turbine or something to save the world. He had the longest mullet hairdo in the world – it was incredible. He has his very own sense of style.

Were you a fan of *The X Factor* before you joined the show?

Totally. The first few shows would draw me in and then I'd be hooked and locked in for the series. I loved it.

How did you feel when you were asked to be one of the new judges?

I was in Australia at the time and people there don't know the show like we do, so it wasn't until I got back to London that I exploded and told all my friends and got properly excited about it. The first day of auditions was just incredible – being in with the judges was amazing. When Simon and Sharon asked for my opinion I was like, 'This is brilliant.' I honestly expected someone to run through the doors and for me to find out that I'd been Punk'd, like on MTV. I thought it was literally the most elaborate Punk'd ever on TV. I was in shock about just being on set.

Who was the first person you told when you got the job?

My parents. I was in Australia doing another of Simon's shows, *Australia's Got Talent*, and my parents don't watch this kind of TV so they were like, 'That's great, what is *The X Factor*?' You would think they would know a lot about the entertainment industry but they have absolutely no idea about some things. They've met

U2 twice at Kylie's shows and they're like, 'Hi. Nice to meet you... What do you guys do?' U2 love it. They think it's cute.

How are all you judges getting on?
We laugh a lot – but all still have our own strong opinions. I felt a bit intimidated and nervous around them at first, and it took me a while to relax because I'm so in awe of them.

We hear that you're planning to give Simon as good as he gives?
Oh yes, I've already started. He's great because he's up for a fight – and I'm the one to challenge him.

How do you feel about the lower age limit now being 14?
It's great. Sharon was saying the other day that 14 is the new 18, and she's so right. These kids have no fear and they just go for it. Some of

the older people who enter need to win so much that it can get ugly, whereas the kids are not like that. And then the people in the middle are just so lippy – but Simon loves that.

Who have been your favourite *X Factor* contestants of all time?
I did like the chicken guy who appeared on the final one year, with his unforgettable version of 'Barbie Girl'. I also liked Leona and Ray from last season a lot. I'm a fan of the music that Ray sang and he was a cute guy. Leona is just fantastic. I wish she'd get more confident though. I'm sure she will, because she's amazing and deserves huge success. It's not very British to have a strict determination, but maybe her time in America will have helped her. I think the more talented people in the UK need support and to trust in their ability. It's not about being cocky, it's about being proud of the talent you have.

ADVICE SECTION

HAVE YOU GOT WHAT IT TAKES?

Are you hoping to be the next big thing? Well before you do anything, read this amazing advice from the judges, the contestants and the voice coach!

Personality

A great personality is just as important as a great singing voice; wallflowers just won't cut it! So be smiley, charismatic and wow the judges.

What advice would you have for anyone going in for the show?
Just be yourselves, and go into the audition room thinking you've got a job to do. Sing from the heart – that's all you can do. Don't come across as too cocky and confident because the judges can tell a mile off if you're being fake. **SHAYNE**

What's the key to a successful *X Factor* auditon?
Be original. We hate it when people come in and try to sound like Stevie Wonder or Michael Jackson. People will try to emulate Mariah Carey or Robbie Williams; they're already out there so we don't need another one. We want someone new. **SIMON**

Who were the most memorable auditionees for you this year?

There have been loads of really good singers. Now we have to find out if they are performers, if they've got personality, if they're easy to work with – we have to find out all these things because it's not just about being a good singer, we need someone who's got everything. It's all about finding what they are made of. Do they just want to be famous or do they want to be in music? They definitely have to want to be in music to work with me. **LOUIS**

What's a good way to impress the judges?

Be nicely dressed and smile! You're there to sell yourself so if you walk in looking nervous and miserable we're instantly put off. It's like going for a job interview – we're looking at everything about you from your shoes to your attitude. So don't be too cabaret and over the top and oversell it. Sometimes less is more. We don't like it if people walk in looking scruffy or if they're there just to appear on TV. You need to want a career in music, not just the fame. **LOUIS**

Confidence

Hold your head high, take a deep breath and
tell yourself you have the confidence to audition
well. Why? Because you have to believe in
yourself, otherwise how will anyone else?!

**Do you know instantly when someone
walks into the audition room if they're a
hit or miss?**
Absolutely, by their body language. You
have to have presence and confidence.
If the auditions weren't filmed
live I would say to a lot of
people as soon as they walk
through the door 'don't bother'.
You need to have something
about you. If you don't have
the confidence to sing in front
of us then you've got no chance.
SIMON

**What's the secret to a
successful audition?**
You've got to make an entrance,
you've got to have confidence
and you've got to have a
personality – something we
can grab onto. And last on the
list, you've got to be able
to perform and sing.
Because if you don't
have the other three, the
fourth one is never going
to work. People can have
good voices, but if the

other elements aren't there, it's not going
to happen. **DANNII**

**What are your tips for a successful
audition?**
You have to walk in with a certain air of
confidence. You can be shy, but you also
have to be confident. And you have to
have likeability and be pleasant because
you can be so turned off if someone is
aggressive. You can pick up a negative
attitude the minute someone walks in the
door. The most important thing you need
is something that pulls people in as soon
as you enter the audition room, and then
you have to win the judges over with your
talent. **SHARON**

**What advice would you have for anyone
thinking about auditioning for *The X
Factor* next year?**
Stay within your comfort zone and don't
just stand there doing nothing. Look like a
star – smile and have confidence. **LOUIS**

**And of course you have to believe in
yourself?**
Totally. Going out in front of millions of
people each week is nerve-wracking, so
you've got to be able to handle it. You've
got to sell yourself to us, and it's a very,
very tough job and you've got to be totally
prepared mentally and physically, and be
dedicated. **LOUIS**

Is there any trick to getting over nerves?
No, but you can openly admit you're
nervous. We know that everybody is,
that's a given. And you make certain
allowances for nerves. People come in
with dry throats and they can't hit the
notes because of it, but you take all of
that into consideration. **SHARON**

Practise, Practise, Practise

It's no good rolling up to auditions and hoping for
the best – practice makes perfect!

**What's the best advice you've been given
during your career?**
I think it's important to be open-
minded, and I've enjoyed doing so
many forms of entertaining, from acting
to singing to musical theatre. I try to
follow my instincts and see what works
for me, but I'm still learning about all
that even now. I think you're constantly
learning, and that's incredibly important.
DANNII

**What is your number one piece of advice
for someone who wants to make it in the
music business?**
You've got to have experience of
performing in front of an audience,
whether it's three people or a thousand.
You have to put the hours in to know how
to get an audience on your side. Some
people come along to auditions and
they've only rehearsed in their bedroom
and that's not good enough. **SIMON**

Perseverance

If at first you don't succeed, keep trying until you do!
The music business is a tough industry; success is not
just going to land in your lap so be prepared to work at it.

What advice do you have for anyone who wants to make it in the music industry generally?
You need to be able to take rejection, and then be able to bounce back again. When we tell people that they're not ready to take things to the next level, they take it as a personal affront and they say to me 'I used to like you'. But it's not about that. This is business and some people just aren't ready. It doesn't mean that I don't like them, but there's a lot riding on these people. Anyone who wants to make it in entertainment has to be able to take rejection because they might just not be right for something at that time. **SHARON**

What advice do you have for anyone who is looking for their big music industry break?
Just keep on trying. I do believe that things happen for a reason. Just keep on working hard and hopefully one day you'll get to where you want to be. Who knows what would have happened if I hadn't won *The X Factor*. But I think I would have carried on trying different things until I had got to where I wanted to go. I was always willing to work hard. **SHAYNE**

Is there one particular ingredient you are looking for in this year's contestants?
I'd like them to be ambitious. I think being ambitious is almost more important than talent. Somebody who will do whatever it takes and just work it, work it, work it! I've seen some absolutely great solo acts with raw talent this year who I'm excited about working with. **LOUIS**

What would you say to someone who wants to make it in the music business generally?
It's really, really hard. It's never been so hard. There are only a few good record companies and unless you stand out from the crowd, you're wasting your time. You have to have great vocals and lots of ambition – you have to have everything. **LOUIS**

Choose Your Song
to Showcase Your Talent

Your song choice is as important as your ability to sing it well. So follow our experts' recommendations and you can't go wrong!

Is it possible to make a terrible singer good?
No, it's like saying to someone 'you have to run the hundred metres in thirty seconds'. You can make someone good better, but you can't make someone totally talentless brilliant. **SIMON**

What songs would you recommend people sing?
It doesn't have to be a well-known song, they should just sing something where the lyrics mean something to them. We decide about thirty seconds into a song whether we like someone or not. They have to make the song their own – we're not looking for karaoke. **LOUIS**

What advice would you have for anyone thinking about auditioning for *The X Factor* next year?
Watch the show and don't come in singing Stevie Wonder or Al Green because there's no way you'll ever do it better than them. **LOUIS**

Are there any songs you never want to hear ever again?
Yes! 'Over the Rainbow', 'Smile', 'Hero' and 'Mustang Sally'. **SHARON**

What do you enjoy most about audition days?
It's really good when somebody first class comes in because then it lights up the room, we all get excited and we all sit there and think 'God, this person could be great, this person could sell records'. It's all about finding somebody with talent and that invigorates us. **LOUIS**

What are the ingredients that you think make up the perfect star?
The perfect star is unique. We don't want any impersonators on this show. Talent, personality and a desire to be the next winner are the key ingredients. **DANNII**

With Yvie Burnett,
The X Factor singing coach

What's your best advice for someone wanting to enter *The X Factor*?

I would say don't enter unless you're completely sure of yourself. Don't just get opinions from your family and friends when you're doing karaoke, maybe go and have a consultation with a vocal coach or do a proper karaoke pub competition where people can judge you. If you don't get past the first round then you've got a bit of a problem if you're expecting to get through a nationwide competition like *The X Factor*.

What if you know you've got talent?

Bear in mind that there's more to it than just having a good voice, and there's more to it than just being a good performer.

In that few moments when you can sell yourself in the audition you want to show that you have everything. You may think you'll be really over the top and emotional, but sometimes all we see is a blank face. It can sound like you're singing your shopping list!

How can you choose a good song to perform?

Well firstly, you need to convey emotion through your eyes so make sure you practise whatever song you choose. You need to know exactly what your song means so do your homework. If you're fourteen or sixteen and you're singing about your husband having an affair after twenty years of marriage, it's obviously not an appropriate song for you. Try and choose a song that you can identify with so you mean what you're singing about as that will always come across.

How can you make sure you get noticed?

You need to make sure you stand out, but not in a comedy way because then you'll stand out for the wrong reasons. Your talent needs to make you stand out. And dress your age – if you're fifty, don't try and dress like you're nineteen!

How can people work out what kind of voice they've got?

Obviously people have favourite artists that they like to listen to, but that doesn't mean your voice will suit their songs. You may be a Mariah fan but your voice may be more suited to KT Tunstall. You need to know that you can sing the notes in the songs you choose to perform. Don't try and attempt something too difficult. Some people think if they can sing a hard song half-decently they'll get through, but that's not the case. It's far better to sing a simple song well than a hard song badly. 'Killing Me Softly' is an ideal song to perform. You can show off your voice

3096

without showing off your faults. If you attempt something too difficult, you'll show off your faults.

What if you're desperate to sing a certain song by your favourite artist?

Think about it first! Once we've coached you and you've got through, maybe you'll get to Mariah Carey's level, but don't try and run before you can walk. If you're Leona Lewis, then fair enough, you can try it. But for every Leona Lewis you've got five hundred Chicos so you've got to audition at your level. We can see potential in you and even if you're not note perfect, we can work on getting you to the level where you could potentially win.

What are the best ways to strengthen your voice?

It's difficult without training because you could do things the wrong way. My best advice is to sing where your voice feels comfortable. If it feels right to you and you can sing the notes, sing it over and over again until you really get to know the song. Hum in the morning when you wake up so you're not straining your voice first thing, and don't overdo it. Your voice is a muscle, and like an athlete trains to run faster, you can train your voice. But if you get tired, stop, the same way a runner would stop if their legs were sore. You can build up your voice yourself as long as you're sensible about it. Don't sing if you've got a cold, but you can hum to get your voice back again. And don't sing if you've been drinking alcohol because by doing that you're drying out your vocal chords.

Are there any songs people should avoid at auditions?

Don't sing Whitney Houston unless you know from experts that you totally trust that you are good enough to do so! Equally, don't sing Queen or Mariah Carey.

Audition Room Dos and Don'ts

DO

Smile! No matter how nervous you feel, a nice cheery smile will make the judges warm to you instantly

Take deep breaths. It will help to calm you before you enter the room

Wear something cool but classy. Wacky isn't always best!

Be polite. Displaying a load of attitude isn't going to get you anywhere

Choose an original song. How many times every year do you think the judges hear '(Sittin' on) The Dock of the Bay' or 'Beautiful' before it gets boring? Erm, not many...

Practise, practise, practise! Have your routine planned out. Do NOT chance it on the day. Make sure you know exactly what you want to do and when

DON'T

Wear a stupid costume. How can you expect to be taken seriously if you're dressed as a zoo animal or a piece of fruit?

Flash the flesh. Getting your bits out won't necessarily get you through the second stage. In fact, it may even put the judges off

Try to emulate anyone else. Doing an impression of Britney's nasally voice or Justin's high-pitched warbles is not big, and it's not clever

Throw yourself around the room like you're possessed. If you're going to dance, make sure you can sing at the same time, and not just sound breathy and weak-voiced

Kiss the judges. Yes, we know it's exciting if you get through, but there's no need to show your appreciation quite that much!

Could You Make it on *The X Factor*?

Have you got what it takes to go all the way? Try our quiz to find out!

1) You see an advert for *The X Factor* auditions in the paper. Do you...
a) Panic and start hyperventilating?
b) Start planning your outfit in your head and start practising your jazz hands?
c) Phone up and get an application form and then make a list of things you need to do to prepare?

2) You're deciding what to sing for your audition. Do you...
a) Not worry too much. You probably won't get through anyway?
b) Go for the biggest hit of the moment as the judges are sure to love it too?
c) Choose something that is well known but not overplayed, so loads of other people won't choose it too?

3) What do you dream about most when you think about being famous?
a) The money
b) Being able to show off 24/7
c) Being able to sing in front of thousands of people

4) How would your friends describe you?
a) Sweet but nervy
b) Wild and crazy!
c) Funny and focused

5) You're deciding what to wear for the audition. Do you...
a) Wear black? You don't want to stand out too much
b) Rush out and buy a neon pink all-in-one and a feather boa?
c) Go for something cool but that doesn't show off too much flesh?

6) If you weren't a singer, what would you like to do?
a) You don't really mind, you just want to earn some money
b) Be a world-famous actress
c) There's nothing you love as much as singing so you'll carry on until you make it!

Mostly As
Scared singer
You would love the chance to be on stage but your nerves often get the better of you and you get too panicky to perform. Relax, take some deep breaths and keep telling yourself how fabulous you are! Oh, and stop worrying about money quite so much...

Mostly Bs
Fame chaser
You love performing, but you don't always take it very seriously and you're all about the glory of fame rather than performing well. You need to make sure you have the talent to make it all the way to back up your obvious confidence!

Mostly Cs
Singing star!
You're serious about wanting to make it as a singer, and your determination and ambition mean you could make it all the way to *The X Factor* finals – and ultimately to Number 1 in the charts!

First published in 2007
by HEADLINE PUBLISHING GROUP

'The X Factor' is a trademark of FremantleMedia Limited and Simco Limited.
Licensed by FremantleMedia Enterprises. www.xfactor.tv

1

A CIP catalogue record for this title is available from the British Library

ISBN 978 0 7553 1690 8

Design by seagulls.net
Printed and bound in Great Britain by Butler and Tanner, Frome

Photographs © Thames/Syco

The publishers would like to thank Sara Lee,
without whose help this book would not have been possible.

Every effort has been made to fulfil requirements with regard to reproducing copyright material.
The author and publisher will be glad to rectify any omissions at the earliest opportunity.

Headline's policy is to use papers that are natural, renewable and recyclable products and
made from wood grown in sustainable forests. The logging and manufacturing processes
are expected to conform to the environmental regulations of the country of origin.

HEADLINE PUBLISHING GROUP
An Hachette Livre UK Company
338 Euston Road
London NW1 3BH

www.headline.co.uk
www.xfactor.tv